ACPL ITE

DISCARDED

Y0-BYU-152

10.17.77

The New York Cab Driver and His Fare

THE NEW YORK CAB DRIVER AND HIS FARE

Charles Vidich

Schenkman Publishing Company
Cambridge, Massachusetts, 02138

Copyright © 1976

Schenkman Publishing Company
3 Mt. Auburn Place
Cambridge, Massachusetts 02138

Library of Congress Catalog Card Number: 74-80370
ISBN: 87073-925-5 cloth
         87073-926-3 paper

Printed in the United States of America

ALL RIGHTS RESERVED. THIS BOOK, OR PARTS THEREOF,
MAY NOT BE REPRODUCED IN ANY FORM WITHOUT
WRITTEN PERMISSION OF THE PUBLISHERS.

Contents

Introduction

In large measure the public's image of the New York City taxi industry has been formulated by the timeless quality of the hack's character. Although the taxi driver poses as a public servant, his actions and his historical reputation in New York have led the public to believe he is all too often working as a crook. In order to introduce the reader to the present image of the New York taxi driver, and the nature of his service, it is necessary to delve into the reputation he has acquired over the past century.

Originally New York was a hansom cab town and each driver worked for himself. There were no great fleets prior to 1907 and in fact only the horse drawn carriage and the electric cab existed in those days. In 1906 the *New York Times* carried a story revealing the nature of the New York hack.

One class of cabmen that are in nearly as bad repute with other cabmen as they are with the public are those known as dock rats. They stand at the steamship piers to pick up strangers that look easy. These dock rats and the men who are in league with disreputable resorts are the curse of decent hackmen. They are free lances that no organization would take in. They lay in wait for people they can overcharge. The dock rats work two to a cab sometimes. When a man leaves a boat, takes a cab and is carried to his destination, the cabman demands two or three times the legal rate. His partner stands by and if there is any hesitation about paying, he says, "Pay up. What 'r'ye waiting for?" In other words, they intimidate the stranger.[1]

By monopolizing the entrances to the city at major piers and terminals, the cab drivers had the public at their mercy. The lack of integrated bus and subway service at the turn of the century serving the demands of rail and boat passengers, created a large market for the taxi driver. In controlling these various transportation systems, the driver could inevitably make the public pay a premium price for his service.

The Plight of the Immigrant

The extortions and crimes of petty larceny indigenous to the operations of the New York docks and passenger terminals left a profound impression on the early immigrants to America. As early as 1913, there were as many as 500,000 aliens passing through the port of New York per year.[2] These immigrants were confronted with a new world of which they knew nothing.

Hackmen, guides, and runners hired by hotels all preyed upon the bewildered immigrants arriving from Ellis Island. These characters forced their services upon the unsuspecting immigrants and then proceeded to take advantage of their victims. It was not uncommon in the early 1900s, when millions of immigrants were rushing to make their homes in America, to find cab drivers, guides, runners and porters victimizing those most in need of their assistance. In those early days cab drivers often entered into conniving relationships with other disreputable public servants in order to put a more effective squeeze on the victim's purse. It was not uncommon for a cab driver to have a working relationship with one or more runners or porters who steered the ignorant immigrant to his cab through various ruses often bordering on outright intimidation.

The immigrant's first contact with America often was accompanied by a lesson in the business ethics of the cab driver. For many immigrants this primary and formative experience strengthened their conviction that they too must learn the ways of American business to achieve success. Indeed, many immigrants entered the taxi profession in its early years, realizing that their original language could be quite effectively used to swindle their former countrymen. The immigrant's problem was clearly stated by the Department of Licenses in 1913 when they released the following news:

The boats from Ellis Island land at the Barge office in Battery Park which is the immigrant's first contact with America. Operating here are a number of porters, expressmen, hackmen and cabmen. These men, through various ruses force their services upon the immigrants, offering to conduct them to their destinations. The bewildered immigrants absolutely ignorant of the city and anxious to do whatever is expected of them, but unable to find out what that is, on account of their ignorance of English, listen eagerly to some one speaking their own language, and are easily drawn into asking questions and accepting directions or guidance. The runners or other agents are not content to charge a reasonable or legitimate rate for their services, but take advantage of the

Battery Park, South Ferry, N.Y. Early immigrants were fair game for the cab hustler. (The Staten Island Historical Society)

immigrant's ignorance of English and of the value of the American money, and of their fear of trouble with the authorities, to extort considerable sums of money from them. In some cases they simply rob them outright.[3]

These hack men were no different from the dock rats operating on the west side piers of Manhattan. However, the ramifications of their actions were more damaging since the immigrant was completely unable to fend for himself. The limited but powerful monopoly of the cab driver over early American immigrants helped to formulate the New York cab driver's notoriety throughout the entire nation. Much of the unpleasantness associated with the initial encounter with American life in New York was attributed to the character and psychology of the New York cab driver.

The dock rats of yesteryear are now the full grown airport rats of today, gouging foreign visitors and New Yorkers alike whenever they are at his mercy. The strong controls which the taxi driver once had over the river terminals and rail terminals of the city continue today at New York's two airports.

Night Hawks

The complementary anti-hero to the dock rat is and was the night hawk. Unlike the dock rat, the night hawk gains his advantage over the public through the cover of darkness and the greater value nighttime gives to taxi service. Indeed in the early days, a caste distinction existed between the day driver and the night driver since the night drivers robbed the public blind with relative immunity. This image is ageless and eternal, describing a practice of hustling that grows bolder as the sun sets. The night hawk learns to prey on the desperate taxi patron, demanding and extorting as much as he thinks the man can deliver. It was said during the 1930s that drivers would circle around and around the block until a pedestrian would finally consent to ride by cab just to avoid the nuisance and aggravation of soliciting hackmen.

With the advent of the motor driven taxi in 1907 fleets began to develop in New York and an increasing number of men became hacks. It was during the 1910s through the early 1930s that the New York fleets became a part of the New York scene and the fleet owner acquired his present image. "Crooked dollar" or "dirty dollar" were names used by hacks to describe what they felt were the negligibly respectable business operations of their employers. The anti-hero hack in essence spread his charm and public renown to the corporate villain. The drivers, in a sense, admire the owner as their partner in crime. Nevertheless, they do not extend praise or felicitations to the owner since the image the owner has acquired is in competition with the nefarious aspirations of the drivers. The competitive individualism of the New York hack not only divides the owner from the driver, it furthermore manages to permanently sever any semblance of camaraderie between fellow drivers. During the 1930s union organizers were as quick to berate the "common whore" hackman as they were to comment on the value of crooked dollars.

For the union organizers, the hack was the last man in the world to be trusted with a union card. The hack was considered the staunchest whore in a stable of selfish pirateering "street cruisers." Indeed the hacks, like the common whore, relinquished their maiden names when they hit the street and began selling their souls for the dollar. The image of the common whore was an obscure and dubious achievement of the hack profession. Unlike the other images the driver has acquired, it never gained the popularity of the anti-hero image of dock rats and night hawks due to its blatant self-defamation. Hackmen have as a rule been able to romanticize and identify with the banditry of their profession. But they have not been able to take pride in the myths which proclaim warfare and banditry among their own ranks. A hack's humor runs rancid when he is cornered into self-apology for the misery and insipid rivalry that proclaims, "each man for himself" or "it's too bad about the union." The common whore may ultimately apologize for destroying the credibility of collective bargaining but deep down he knows that the Union man is no different from the crooked dollar. He might say, "Why they're just out to hustle us for a bit of money too," or "How many ways can we split this pie anyway?" For the hack, the union boss is just a party to the collusion that takes money out of his pocket. "I don't need no union if all it's going to do is shortchange my paycheck," is the response of many drivers today. They would rather forego the formalities of collective bargaining and get down to where the real bargains are to be found—on the street. The driver's conception of his partners stems from an underlying attitude of, "Count me out; I don't need so many partners."

Closed Lines and Taxicab Jockeys

During the days when the hansom cab was the only cab service in New York, the hack was required to operate from public or private stands. With the introduction of the taxicab in 1907 this mode of operation underwent certain alterations. Business began improving for the cab industry, reflecting a new demand for its services. In turn, the crooked dollars of the early years of the industry established private contracts with terminals and other businesses producing large volumes of customers that monopolized the taxi market. This arrangement between terminals or hotels had arisen as early as 1834 when the city allowed special Hackney carriages to enter the business only if they operated from private property such as a hotel, steamship landing or dock.[4]

Naturally as the city of New York grew from a village in the early 1800s to a bustling urban center in the early twentieth century, these private arrangements between terminals and cab companies became quite valuable. In fact they became so valuable that private concessions during the early years of the taxi industry were much more valuable than the public hack stands offered by the city. Cruising the streets was virtually unheard of when the taxicab was first introduced, although the growing demand for taxi service from 1910 onward soon prompted the growth of cruising cabs. By 1920, cruising the streets for fares became a lucrative means of making a living—a development which cut into the use of public or private stands and made the taxicab a major traffic problem. However, certain private hack stands continued to be valuable assets during the following years despite the increase in cruising.

The most lucrative stands during these years were controlled by major fleet companies such as Terminal Transportation Systems and Yellow Taxicab Corporation. These two companies controlled Grand Central Terminal and Pennsylvania Railroad Station taxi service from 1921 to 1950.[5] For those drivers fortunate enough to belong to the right company or strong enough to proclaim squatters rights, the closed lines of the private stand offered valuable monopolies. Drivers not belonging to the company owning the stand were closed out of the line with force if it became necessary. Oftentimes drivers who disobeyed the law of the brotherhood owning the stand would find their tires slashed and their vehicle smashed if they ventured into line. Independent drivers and brotherhoods of loosely affiliated fleet drivers often obtained the same monopolistic controls over public hack stands through the use of violence and intimidation. However, for these drivers, their closed lines lacked the same monopolistic value as the ones controlled by the larger taxi fleets operated on private property because they were forced to rely on intimidation and violence in order to remain in control. Cab drivers belonging to these brotherhoods were not to be fooled with. Oftentimes these men were hardened criminals, posing as hacks, using the taxicab as their vehicle for committing crime. Those drivers foolish enough to enter into their hack stand could expect the worst. If they left without bodily injury they were considered fortunate, or so it was said in the early years of the industry.

Even now in Brooklyn and the Bronx it is said that oldtimers will tell you, "What are you doing in this line? You're not going to make any money here." Although the days of the closed line are through, the mythology lives on as testament to the rancour and strife endemic to the brotherhood of hacks.

Another technique employed by drivers was to take a partner in crime and put the squeeze on the passenger's purse. Taxicab jockeys, as they were called, rode the running boards of the old taxis offering to sell the cab to the patron willing to pay the highest tip. This practice was quite severe in the early days of the industry when people relied on the taxi to make connections between the ferries to New Jersey and the train station. The *New York Times'* quotation on the dock rats of 1906 accurately describes the conniving alliance of the dock rat and his partner, the taxicab jock. Jockeys were barred from entering into a business relationship with their disreputable partners, the dock rats, in 1913; however, they continued their activities as long as the automobile manufactures produced taxis with running boards. Although the modern driver has no partner to intimidate his passenger, he will on occasion take on a outside partner in another line of business to bolster his income. As a steerer, the cabby often suggests restaurants, hotels, whores, gambling parlours, dope deals, etc., which might interest the passenger. In return for the business, his partner pays him a head charge or weekly fee for his work. The steerer, unlike the taxicab jockey, reflects a slightly different concern. The steerer is concerned with expanding his business interests, whereas the jockey merely wants to corner the taxi market. The practice of steering passengers to certain places of ill repute is uncommon, yet it forms the basis of the hack personality as the public conceives it. It is assumed that the cab driver will know where to take the passenger if he so desires certain business or services otherwise unadvertised in the yellow pages. By implication, the myth persists that the cabby not only knows the New York underground and its workings but that he is in alliance with it.

The myths of the industry are also its realities. The hyperboles and innuendoes of raconteur hacks have achieved fame within the profession, but beyond their entertainment value, they have served to mold a style of life and an occupational character for the driver. The myths draw the hacks into romantic undying caricatures of themselves. The hack on the one hand revels in his own notoriety and on the other he pleads exemption from the malice and public hostility incurred through the dissemination of the myths of his profession. Ideally he would like to be on both sides of the argument. He wishes to defend himself amongst his chums as being no "boss' sucker," yet he is quick to clarify the distinction between himself and the rest of those sordid drivers "giving me a bad name" when he sweet talks his fare. The driver as usual is true to nobody or nothing. If it is to his advantage, he will knock his profession and disclaim any love for its conniving mythological motifs. A hack's love for his profession is second to his love for money. "If you can't make a buck off it, what good is it?" Surely attitudes of this kind lead to no deep loyalty amongst the ranks of hack men.

The Language of the Cab Driver

Like the mythology of the industry, the cab driver's vocabulary reflects the values he shares with his peers. The vocabulary of the cabby is action oriented and many of the words and phrases are predatory in nature. It is a language of combat and coercion, including such words as "bandits," "crashing," "steerer," "gestapo," "buckers," and phrases like "stiff you," "double up," "common whores," and "break the ice," as outstanding examples of their jargon.[6] There are virtually no positive words in their vocabulary. Rather, the words of the cab driver grow from his concern with sabotage, subterfuge, and self-mockery. Getting caught violating the hack rules, cheating on the boss or passenger, competing with gypsy cabs and fellow drivers, and avoiding the clutches of the police are the breeding grounds for their vocabulary.

The structure of the fleet operation appears corrupt and nefarious when one learns that fleet dispatchers are called, "Mr. Big" or "Inside Men" and the owner, as described in the original myths is called, "crooked dollar" or "dirty dollar." Nevertheless, such words as dock rats, water rats, airport rats, and night hawks strike equal fear in the passenger as the former words do in the driver.

Some of the words are strictly concerned with the purely aboveboard economics of the industry, such as: "fare rate," "break the ice," "initial drop," "dead heading," "bonus pay," and "bookings."[7] However, the more descriptive and eloquent feelings and phrases of the profession are one and the same with the hustling spirit of the job. Sabotage, deception, and illegality suggest the climate from which the vast majority of their words arise. In fact, what are listed in the Hack Rules and Regulations governing public hacks as violations, are within the jargon of the driver's suitable behavior.[8] As a result, their jargon can almost be read as a paraphrase of the crimes prohibited by law. Such expressions as "flag up," "crashing," "bussing," "doubling up," "flag down no passenger," "riding the ghost," "riding the arm," "on the arm," "arm job," "expressage," "flat rate" and untold others describe the actions of hackmen.[9]*

For the most part these words are rarely heard except by judges and cabmen. Indeed, many of the drivers are unwilling to openly relate their

*For an explanation of the drivers' jargon, see the Glossary.

experiences to other cabmen, feeling, as is often the case, that there is no love lost between cab drivers. To openly avow criminal activity is a difficult decision. One never knows if there might be a cab driver listening who might take offense or merely a man who works honestly and might become irritated by the ease with which many drivers make more money. In fact, open conversation of the actions described by the words above often triggers a moral battle among drivers. Although their words refer to their cheating of passengers, the boss or other drivers, they interpret all their actions as means of cheating back on the boss, to get even for what he has done to them in the past or for what they think the world owes them. Cab drivers, in a sense, are united in opposition to the fleet owner and can refer to their illegal activity as just so many ways of dealing with economic repression. As long as there is a justification for cheating, the cabby feels his vocabulary as an extension of his camaraderie, however tenuous it may be. Nevertheless, when the driver cheats others besides the boss, as he invariably does, he finds himself in a precarious position talking about it.

With the growth of the private livery car service in the ghettoes, New York cab drivers have coined several new phrases and have redefined some old words to fit their latest competitors. All of the words are disparaging, although some of the terms applied to the private liveries are also applied to the medallion industry. Gypsy is the most prominent word used to describe the livery services although more eloquent drivers have called them the cattle boats from Puerto Rico or Mama and Papa Gypsies. Descriptive language relating to the liveries has not developed to any marked degree, due to the general false assumption that it is a passing phenomenon. So far the standard English four letter epithets have precluded the emergence of any new words to describe the private livery and gypsy operations.

The driver's use of the word "hot seat" to describe the passenger detection system installed in fleet taxis gives the distinct impression that somebody is getting burned.† In a sense, the hot seat implies more than just a cute description of an electrical fixture—it is a metaphor for the death of the hustler. For in fact it is not just the passenger who is getting burned but the cheating driver. The hot seat in effect describes the system of justice within the taxi industry. And as any driver will tell you, it isn't functioning very well.

The militant side of the cabby's diction is expressed in his portrayal of the fleet owner's detective squad as the "gestapo." Their existence and tactics are an outrage to the cab driver who generally feels nobody should have authorized these "goons" to interfere with their work. Cabbies in fact look upon the supervision of the industry as an expression of the repressive

---

†An explanation and description of the "hot seat" is given in Chapter 1.

tactics of the boss. "These hired guns can do us no good, they've been paid to find trouble, so they'll make trouble," is the gist of the driver's view. Gestapo is also a borrowed word and like the word "hot seat" it points to the bitterness and discord between the driver and his boss.

Violence and hostility gush from the driver's language. Business is transformed into combat, friendship into subterfuge, integrity into self-mockery, and existence into a cosmic form of coercion. The drivers' search for justice and a reprieve from the depravities of the profession has found little expression in their jargon. Their language expresses the constant competition of business and the combat of personal relations.

1

Beating The System

The Cab Driver At Work

Fare Game: Coping with the Passenger

In order to survive in the hack profession, a cabby, out of necessity, must learn the tools of the profession. In the cab business there is no sitting back, waiting, squandering time, filling the week with subtle forms of job subterfuge. Under the commission system there is no money to be made simply waiting for the appearance of the weekly paycheck. This does not mean that New York cabbies are better workers than workers in salaried positions. Quite the contrary, the commission system creates an atmosphere of instability regarding who is boss and who reaps the profits. Although fleet owners unceasingly search for methods of detecting cheaters on the job, there is virtually no way this can be done when the driver possesses the freedom of mobility provided by the taxi. As a result of this freedom, the cabby quickly realizes that any and all tricks he uses to make money for the boss can be used in a much better fashion to make money for himself.

The commission system places the burden upon the cab driver of producing an income. Faced with the fear of economic disaster, cheating becomes the basic economic crutch to sustain many a cabbie's income and motivate his enthusiasm. He alone determines what income he will bring home, notwithstanding the fluctuations of the market. Under these pressures of survival, cabbies have managed to relieve themselves of some of the burden of proof involved in making a living. By whittling down the time spent working for the boss rather than for themselves, the cabbies manage to increase their income without "taxing" their energy. Although the freedom of the job causes problems for one who is unsure of his ability to make a living, it also provides an incentive to make more than is allowed by the union contract. The desire to cheat, or to make money by unethical means is strictly speaking an irrational outgrowth of the profession.[1] Nobody is cheating the cabbie; nevertheless, he finds it necessary to cheat his boss and oftentimes his customers. To get more for doing less is a tired and dogged axiom of capitalism as well as the New York taxi industry. The dollar sign becomes the burden of proof for all hack friendships.

The intellectual tools of the hack profession are logical extensions of the will to survive under these cutthroat conditions. In effect, his skills are directed toward maximizing his income and minimizing his partner's income. Cabbies are notorious for hustling passengers for an extra buck. Yet very few people are aware of the concerns which form his occupational skills. In a sense the ideal conditions underlying Darwin's survival of the fittest prescribe the behavior of cab drivers in New York. Their skills are directed toward achieving unfettered conditions in the street. This would mean no cops, no lights, no crime, no dead heading (Note: Whenever a cabbie drives without a passenger in the cab, it is described as dead heading) and no partners. In actuality the cabby can never get exactly what he wants although his purpose is to realize a situation as near as possible to the ideal described above. The tools of the hack profession as well as its mythology reflect the following concerns: the synchronized light system, the passenger screening and bargaining system, the meter (which in effect represents the driver's agreement with the boss and the union) and the operating patterns of the police surveillance squads. These are where the tools of the profession come into play. Each of these areas presents a problem to the cabby which in turn creates a counter-system of skills, tricks and tecniques by which he is able to survive in the taxi industry.

In part, his occupational values are merely complementary to the larger moral fabric of the fleet owner and the union. Nevertheless there exist specific barriers to economic success which force New York cabbies to develop skills beyond those required by their patrons. These skills are part of a larger enterprise called "beating the system" and represent the essential tools of the hack in plying his trade.

Synchronized Light System

Since time is an essential consideration to a driver who lives solely off his commissions, New York hacks find they are forced to contend with the problems of traffic congestion and the synchronized light system in order to save time and make more money.

A cab driver has to know when and where to be in order to procure his fare. In New York, if a hack does not know where to go to flow with the traffic and where to take the necessary short cut, all he'll manage to produce is a headache for himself. The synchronized lights of New York in a sense transform the traffic department's rules into a large scale game of pinball. The hack must know which streets flow fastest and which don't. A more favorable pattern of lights can mean making one more fare by the end of the day. Since time is such a vital element in the hacking profession, a red light can often be nothing more than a barrier to making a living. In many areas of Brooklyn, Bronx or Queens, stopping at a red light will not serve to promote business, as it often does on busy streets in midtown Manhattan. When a hack expects a certain area of the city to be good for fares. he will observe all the legal etiquette of stopping at a red light. Why not? It is at red lights that many of the fares are procured. A red light offers the hack a chance to advertise his presence without being guilty of double parking or holding up traffic. Nevertheless the hack's compliance with the traffic rules extends no further than their personal utility. They see no more in a red light than their pocketbook dictates. Some drivers are constant light runners while others will slow down a block away in order to catch the light. Oddly enough neither driving style works better than the other, although both styles share the same end—procuring fares. Some drivers think that the next fare is going to be just ahead of that rapidly changing green light so that if they don't hurry, some undeserving hack coming off a side street will beat them to their fare. Other drivers are of the opinion that the fare will come to them and feel fares are more inclined to grab a stopped cab than one careening down the street at 40 miles per hour.

There is little firm evidence that suggests one style of hacking is better than the next. In fact, many drivers develop a flexibility in their hacking styles to adjust to the competition from other taxis or gypsy cabs. If a pack of taxis are all intent on racing the synchronized light system of 1st Avenue from one end of Manhattan to the other, some drivers will hold back from

the lead of the pack and attempt to pick up stray fares who are too intimidated by this show of strength. Hustling does not always mean going
faster than the driver in front of you. One plays it by experience. Many
factors such as the time of day, the driver's location within the city, and
the level of competition determine his driving style. A red light often spells
green when a driver finds himself in East Harlem at two in the morning with
a large band of kids rapidly converging on his taxi. Similary, it does not
serve any useful purpose to catch every light on Brooklyn's Flatbush Avenue if the driver is in a hurry to get back to Manhattan.

A hack's attitude toward the synchronized light system is extremely
utilitarian; "if I'm not making money by stopping at this light, then why
stop?" However, when the driver has a fare, red lights are taken care of by
the cost of waiting time as it is determined by the meter.

When the taxi is empty, the driver can only look at a red light as a possible
investment. The extra minute spent at the light might produce a fare that
would otherwise have been overlooked. The decision to catch the light rests
on the hack's knowledge of the area and its people, culled from years of
experience driving in the city. Running the light represents a risk to a cabby
but this risk becomes part of the operating procedure of his work. It is rare,
indeed, for a hack to wait at a light where there is no chance of nabbing
a fare, no cross traffic and no cop in sight.

A sensible driver knows how to take advantage of the synchronized lights
so as to extend his visibility on the streets and amplify the area and the
potential patrons he might serve. Cruising the street for fares can not be
separated from the workings of the synchronized light system as it operates
throughout the city. Drivers must take into account the effect of the light
system on their ability to travel from one place to another within the city.
The light system at best allows a driver to sometimes travel 28 miles an hour
for distances of five or six miles without stopping.

The synchronization of lights has been developed by the traffic department to favor north-south patterns of travel in Manhattan. As a result,
north-south patterns of cruising on the island of Manhattan allow for the
greatest coverage of space in the shortest time. East and west streets, on the
other hand, rarely have a patterned lighting system. It becomes part of the
personal cruising style of each driver to know which streets by chance,
resemble or sometimes operate on a near synchronized lighting pattern. The
major east and west thoroughfares through Central Park, and feeder arteries for the midtown tunnel, 59th street bridge, Manhattan and Brooklyn
bridges all operate on a synchronized light system to accommodate their
larger volumes of traffic.

The beauty of crosstown cruising as opposed to cruising along the avenues is that the driver is able to maximize the time rather than the space he covers. However, crosstown cruising can only be an aid in heavily congested commercial and business areas. Rarely will a driver be found cruising on crosstown streets other than in the midtown or central business district of Manhattan. Although drivers do use crosstown streets outside of the central business district, it is primarily to circle back to home turf. Much like a dog that constantly comes back to that old tree to claim it as his own, the hack spends most of his time cruising his favorite spots.

Screen System

Assuming the driver has dealt with New York's red lights and accommodated himself to some choice hunting grounds for "fare" game, he does not want to find himself totally at the mercy of whatever person hails his cab. In theory any fare is a profitable fare, although in practice it sometimes works out differently. Not every fare is going to take the hack where he wants to go. That is by no means a small consideration when a cabby finds himself with an empty cab after dropping off his fare in the deserts of East New York or Bedford Stuyvesant. A cab driver possesses as a necessary part of his intellectual arsenal, a screening system by which he passes judgment on the merits and demerits of his potential fare. There are many considerations that can be used to "once over" the potential passenger. Not all drivers are able or willing to spend the time to give a home interview to the passenger. For the most part, each driver develops his own standard criteria of "grading" a fare. Some drivers, naturally mix a certain personal blend of paranoia into their screen system, which is understandable given the long history of robberies in the taxi industry. One driver who has been driving for over 14 years said:

> You can never be certain of the passenger. You can't tell. I'll give you a little story. I picked up this guy with a tuxedo and from what they were talking it seems him and his girl friend just came from a wedding. They took me into Brooklyn, just dropped the girl off and when I took the guy to the place where he wanted, the next thing I know he pulled a 45 on me and robbed me. So you can't tell what's coming off. There's no guessing whatsoever. I had the biggest tip from a guy who was dressed worse than a bowery bum.

Although a hack can never be sure about the person he picks up he usually feels it is safer to pick up a fare in a busy midtown street than in Bedford Stuyvesant. In a sense the driver uses his cruising ritual as just an extension of his passenger screening system. A driver who has a fairly rigid cruising pattern fixed to the midtown Manhattan area is more than likely to have a rigid screening system for passengers he encounters on a return from a long haul out of Manhattan. Although no driver is completely rigid in his criteria for evaluating a passenger, most consider the following factors: the quality of the environment, or the neighborhood, the social and economic status of the area in which the potential passenger stands, the people he is hanging out with, his race or nationality, how he is dressed, where he is standing, and in what direction he is hailing the cab. Usually no driver will spend the time to evaluate a fare by all those factors. In fact, any driver who actually would take the time to consider all the possible evidence is a damn scared hack.

Hacks who discriminate against residents of outlying boroughs of New York generally have two motives. They are either of the opinion that a fare outside of New York proper is less likely to be destined for a commercial area or is more likely to be a potential gunman out to fleece his pockets. These feelings are by no means unjustified. The major areas in which cab drivers get robbed are in black and Puerto Rican ghettoes outside of the heart of Manhattan.

By curtailing his cruising pattern, a hack can avoid cruising for fares in suburban neighborhoods such as Queens and Brooklyn where the private automobile and gypsy cab are his primary form of competition. If perchance a driver does spot a fare on a return trek from the fringes of an outer borough, he may often consider the direction in which the fare is headed as a possible "tip off" to where he might be going. This is by no means a foolproof check. Passengers are known to stand in certain preestablished heavily used taxi corridors of the city to be sure of catching a cab. In doing so the passenger may walk well away from the direction in which he wishes to travel in order to secure a cab. It is common knowledge that cab drivers use major avenues feeding into Manhattan more so than they use circumferential streets or avenues to the midtown area of Manhattan. As a result, the driver knows that the passenger knows where to hail him. This means that among the people standing on a street leading toward Manhattan are certain individuals standing there with the sole purpose of snaring them to go in the opposite direction. The person standing on the inbound side of the street late at night is well aware that a hack has no other goal than to return to the busy night life of Manhattan. Consequently that person stands on the side of the street the cab passes to catch the cabby's attention as well as to gain the faith of the cabby that he truly is a person headed in the same direction.

The game of outwitting the New York hack is not an easy one. Potential passengers may indeed pass all the tests by standing on the right side of the street and pointing themselves in the same direction as the cabby, yet they fail to catch his attention. When a hack ignores a hail that by all rights is a "safe bet," it usually means that he has caught a certain clue in the man's behavior that leads him to second guess the true motives of his potential fare. An overly frantic lunging gesture to hail the cab or the sight of an empty taxi which presumably passed by the same man are enough to signal to the driver that something is afoul. Unfortunately, the passenger who is more desperate for a taxi than most people and is destined for an area difficult to reach by anything other than an automobile, will find that hacks are often intimidated by frantic gestures if they know that it is indicative of the passenger's destination. These overly excited gestures tend to be positively ignored if the hack is driving the night shift and is passing through a black ghetto where three heavyset blacks in their twenties are standing waiting for a cab. Although the cabby may wonder where they are headed, his second thought, "Who really cares," passes the final verdict.

Many passengers will not be served for the simple reason that they travel in a group of four or five. When a hack has to open the front door of his cab to properly seat all his passengers, he may very well feel he is taking an unwanted risk. Since all fleet taxis are required to have bullet resistant partitions, drivers have become accustomed to a shield protecting them from their passenger. Once a hack has drawn a literal and a psychological barrier between himself and his passenger, any breakdown between passenger and driver becomes a threat to the hack's sense of security. Today, fleet drivers have become so accustomed to partitions, which the union required taxi fleets to install in the latter part of 1968, that few cabbies will now pick up more than three passengers. If perchance a hack complies with a hail, he relies on the bullet resistant partition as the final screen between himself and his fare.

Without a doubt, blacks and Puerto Ricans are at a distinct disadvantage in hailing a cab. It is a known fact to cab drivers that blacks and Puerto Ricans are the most likely to be taxi robbers. Indeed nearly 70 percent of all the taxi robberies in Manhattan during 1971 were in the uptown area known as Harlem. A similarly high percentage of taxi robberies has been associated with the black and Puerto Rican areas of Bronx, Queens, and Brooklyn. Although hacks might not be aware of the trends in taxi robberies, as the police are, they are able to learn quite quickly from the first hand accounts of other drivers who have been robbed or through having the unfortunate personal experience happen to them. As the most recent immigrants to the city of New York, blacks and Puerto Ricans are the least trusted. It is only under heavy qualification that hacks will consider a black man as their fare. Godfrey Cambridge, a well known black comedian is one of many who have learned first hand how the New York hack operates. In March of 1974 the *New York Times* carried the following story:

The black comedian Godfrey Cambridge used to get mileage out of a routine in which he offered a "rent-a-white" service to blacks having difficulty making white cab drivers stop to pick them up. But on December 5, 1969 Mr. Cambridge charged, he had the unfunny experience of being dragged more than a dozen blocks by a taxi after the driver had refused to take him as a passenger.

This type of incident may not be the usual occurrence but it indicates the extremes to which some drivers may go in order to avoid picking up black people.

The least used index of a passenger's acceptability comes into play when the driver is torn between the *contradictory* information his fare presents. A black man who is also young translates into two menacing signs for the hack. Yet if the man happens to be accompanied by a well-dressed woman, especially if she is white and coming from a prominent midtown hotel, the driver will disregard the first two warnings and accept the fare. In essence, the screening system is nothing more than a highly developed game of probability. The hack says to himself, "What are the chances of getting ripped off by a black man and a white woman coming out of a good hotel?" He'll probably think the black man is less of a risk to his life and money when accompanied by a woman than he would be if he were alone. Although the couple may get the hack's initial approval there is still the chance that they may be going to an area of the city at a time of day when the hack can afford to be choosy. This situation leads the driver to his final ploy in the screening system. Before the passenger can get ever so slightly near the door handle of the cab, the cabby is certain to question the whereabouts of their final destination before he unlocks the rear door. "Ask questions first and open the door later," is the heart of the screening philosophy. The exchange need go no further than a peremptory plea for service when the driver decides he and his passenger share no common ground in the discussion.

It is only natural that drivers try to minimize the number of times they are forced to disqualify a potential fare. The screening system can only be an asset if the driver is able to employ it to increase his chances of making more money. If the screening becomes excessively rigid, hacks will find themselves at an economic disadvantage.

Bargaining System

The screening in a sense never stops. The cabby is always careful that he hasn't misjudged the moral character of his fare. Nevertheless, the potential economic consequences of the trip fall into the background as the hack appraises the financial liquidity of his patron. He need not be overly concerned whether his fare is a taxi robber as long as he scrutinized him before letting him in and the taxi is equipped with a partition. Nevertheless, the partition can only serve as a mild deterrent to holdups. The true effect is to alienate the driver from his patrons. The barrier between the driver and the passenger is a real one, whereas prior to the advent of the partition in 1968,[3] it was purely imaginary.

The partition in effect says that the driver is afraid whether he or she is or is not. This is a permanent screen which has certain economic repercussions for the driver when it comes time to get paid or receive a tip.

Regardless of whether the driver's intentions are honest or not, one of his first thoughts is, "What is this guy good for?" A New York hack is all too willing to bargain for the price of the ride if he thinks it is worth his while. This practice is strictly illegal. According to the rules, the price of the fare is determined by the meter. Nevertheless, the cabby does not always consider the meter as his only means for making the passenger pay. In his opinion there are two choices: either to be honest and work for the big tip or to negotiate the price of the ride off the meter. In the first case the bargain is struck in the tip while in the latter the driver attempts to bargain for the whole ride. The object of the bargain in essence is to maximize the amount of unaccountable money passing through his hands. Fleet drivers, unlike owner drivers, are held accountable for a percentage of all the bookings made on the meter. As a result, every driver is concerned with minimizing the amount of total money that is actually registered on the meter while maximizing the total receipts that go directly into his pocket.

In the bargain, the driver cheats the Internal Revenue Service out of its share of the money and limits the number of dollars the fleet owner receives without being held accountable as a "low booker." Within the context of the bargaining procedure, the driver is usually wary of striking an off-the-meter bargain with a potential stool pigeon. If there is any doubt as to whether the passenger shares the same moral values in business as himself, he will either abandon the attempt or proceed to ferret out the feeling of his patron regarding the deal. Oftentimes the cabby will approach the subject of the bargain in a roundabout fashion. Instead of saying, "I'll take you there for $2" he might say, "What is the ride worth to you?" In this way he learns quickly whether the passenger is willing to become an accomplice in an off-the-meter negotiation without directly jeopardizing his hack license or his job.

Naturally, there are many hacks who could not care in the slightest whether their passenger shares the same values. These are the super hustlers of the profession. Against them there is little the passenger can do but notify the police.

Griping for Tips

The tragedy of the taxi driving profession is that tips are still the bread and butter of the job. Nearly 40 percent of all the money made by New York cab drivers comes from tips. Tips are the intangible item in the earnings of a driver, yet they represent the most important part of his income. If a New York hack can successfully make 40 percent of his income on tips, he is actually making more than that amount since only 20 percent of his total income is held tax accountable as tips by the Internal Revenue Service. The present economic recession and recent fare hikes of 1971 and 1974 have done much to hurt the earnings made off tips. When times are bad and fleet owners petition for a fare hike, the first item taxi patrons forget is the tip. Thus the cab driver often will absorb a great deal of the loss in the reduction in his tip. "You might be able to afford a cab if you don't tip the driver," is the essence of the passenger's reaction to a fare hike.

Naturally cab drivers have learned what types of people are good tippers and what types are not. There is a general consensus amongst drivers that out of towners can not be counted on when it comes time to get the tip. One cabbie put it this way:

> Out of towners are cheap. Here in New York City you have an awful lot of people working on tips. The cab drivers, the waiters, the porters, the doormen —all working on tips. If they don't get a tip they don't go home with a good salary. Hey and when a person's got a family to support and a person doesn't tip him it hurts. And the thing is these out of towners are so used to where they live they don't tip. Or if they do put a tip they undertip the people.

Although not all drivers will agree on what makes a good tipper and what class, sex or ethnic groups tip the best they all operate with preconceived notions about who tips and who doesn't. Many drivers feel that New Yorkers are "set tippers" since they know exactly what the fare is going to be and exactly how much they ought to give as a tip. However on the subject of women, blue collar workers, and minority groups there is considerable variation of opinion. Here's how one veteran driver looks at passengers:

> Only the blue collar workers overtip. They're the best tippers around. No matter what nationality they are. Women on the other hand are split half and half. Just like a woman. You take a woman—in my opinion is a light head. One time's she's cheap and the next time she's expensive. And that's it. You never know with a woman what she's going to do. Hey I had a woman get in the cab and leave a 15,000 dollar mink stole in the cab. She was drunk as all get out but she went into a store to get something. I know she was too drunk to

remember my name or number or anything and I could have rolled right off with that thing. Couldn't I? Yet when I came to the end of the ride she started to yell at me that I took her the long way. So go ahead. She trusts me with her 15,000 dollar stole and yet she yells at me that I took her the long way to her house. That's a woman for you. They tip the same way they think.

When it comes to the people that live on Fifth Avenue, Eastend Avenue, Park Avenue, Westend Avenue—let's be practical about it. They've got a doorman to tip, any nightclub they walk into there's always someone putting their hands out. How much could they tip? What I don't like about them is that the guy that opens the door for them, they hand him a buck and the cab driver—all they hand him is a quarter. This gets me. I did more of a service than the guy that just walked over and opened the door for them. That's the only thing I got against those people. In my opinion they overtip the wrong people.

Another cabby was briefer about who tips: "As an ethnic group the Puerto Ricans are the best tippers. But as for women — who knows. Well maybe if you get a fat girl or a waitress or a beautician, she'll give you a good tip." Naturally cab drivers are apt to try a little harder for a tip when they know the person they are talking to fits their model of a good tipper.

There are three basic theories drivers use in bargaining for a good tip. The first is based on the premise, "if I can make my fare feel sorry for me and my kind, he might be more philanthropic when it comes time to tip." This species of New York cab drivers will engage in conversations that generally have the underlying theme of how times are bad and the recession hasn't spared anyone including the cabby. Oftentimes this technique of inducing the patron to tip borders on outright intimidation which causes many people to be truly afraid of giving a cabby less than 20 percent of the price of the fare. In fact one cabby said,"I always tell out of towners, of course it's customary to tip 20 percent." Indeed, an irate and brazen hack often accomplishes his bargaining purpose through sheer gall and nerve.

To many drivers the above method of securing a tip is extremely repugnant. This latter group of drivers are of the opinion that no form of ingratiation whatsoever is any more productive than any other. It is the feeling of drivers of this group that talk is useless as an aid to securing a tip since most passengers are merely going to give a standard tip anyway. One driver put it this way, "For fourteen years of cab driving—I talked to people, I didn't talk to people and all I got was a set tip. That's it." These drivers often resign themselves to this point of view and blame the lack of dialogue between the driver and the passenger on the presence of the bullet resistant partition which has made it nearly impossible for the driver to converse with his passenger. The strengthening of the distance between the passenger and the driver works two ways. Although it offers the driver a minimal form of self-protection, it also allows the passenger the anonymity of a small tip. For this reason many drivers berate the value of the partition. However, the value of the partition ultimately comes down to the question of whether the cabby values his security more than he values a big tip from his fare. The compartmentalization of the interior of the taxi has depersonalized the service provided by the taxi, placing it at the same level of personal contact found between a subway conductor and his passengers. The passenger for the most part is perfectly content to maintain this form of anonymity. The less contact he develops with his driver, the less he is indebted for the service rendered.

The partition had its origin in the horse-drawn carriage days, and actually became a part of the early styling of the first motor driven taxis. The partition in those days, unlike the present one, had an entirely different purpose. In the early New York taxi of the turn of the century, the partition represented the class distinction between the hack and his patrons. It was more a symbol of the division between the classes than it was a defense of the driver from the possible unwanted assaults of his passenger.[4] The early taxi riding clientele were much more wealthy. While the hackney carriages and early taxis of New York, as a result, catered to the class and status symbols of the clientele they primarily served, the present partition has an entirely different history and origin. It dates back to the early fifties when the police department suggested that partitions might be installed to prevent robbery. Nevertheless, most owners did not install partitions until the union in 1968 demanded adequate protection for their membership. In the fall of 1968 the police department required all fleet owned taxis to be equipped with a partition. This obsession with security was reinforced in the spring of 1971 when the police department mandated the installation of bullet resistant partitions to replace the preexisting plexiglass partition, which offered little physical or psychological security to the cab driver. The present partition offers nothing more than the previous one except in so far as the robber believes it to be an effective barrier to crime. As a spokesman for the police department stated: "The partition we have specified calls for bullet resistant, not bullet proof. Don't think a partition is intended to prevent a bullet, because we have never had anybody shoot through a partition. It was mainly to alleviate the fear of the drivers."

The spectacular increase in taxi robberies over the last few years is a testament to the robber's disbelief in the effectiveness of this partition. Ironically, there have been more robberies since the installation of the partition in 1968 than in all of the previous years. In a sense, the more the driver has become alienated from his passenger, the more he has felt the need for protection. In turn, his need for protection has caused him to depersonalize his relationships with his passengers, fearing possible robbery. In the extreme it has meant that drivers have refused to serve many peoples and sectors of the city for fear of robbery or death.

The partition, furthermore, has made it psychologically easier for the robber to deal with a cab driver. He is no longer stealing from a man trying to make a living but from a symbol of distrust. The motivations to steal from a medallioned cab driver become easier to justify when it becomes apparent that he fears to serve certain areas of the city.

One older woman cab driver has a very sensitive appraisal of the partition. She stated:

> I felt the partition would create a very real barrier between people where previously there were only imaginary ones and I spent a lot of time trying to dissipate the imaginary ones by relating to the people individually. A partition says loudly that the driver is afraid whether he or she is or not. I am largely not and work against developing unnecessary fears. Fear works against you in any case.[6]

In the face of the near insurmountable challenge of speaking through a bullet resistant partition an increasing number of drivers are abandoning the third and historically most time honored way of procuring a large tip. At one time a driver could earn a good tip by proving to his patron that he was not one of those much talked about con men masquerading as a hack. The newspaper mythology of the hack profession served as the starting point from which an honest hack could prove his integrity. If a hack could successfully prove he was not related to the pirateering element of the profession, that often proved to be enough to reward him with a generous tip. Oddly enough in New York a cabby does not actually need to perform any positive service other than the trip itself to deserve a tip. In fact one cab driver suggests that any time a driver does any special favors for which he is not reimbursed, the passenger should be wary. He tells his story as follows:

> The guy gets in and said take me to Far Rockaway. I said, "O.K." Why not. It's a good fare. I take him out to Far Rockaway and he says at 12th street, "It's just another couple of blocks." So I say "That's Inwood. I don't go out of the city limits—that's a flat rate." He said, "Come on. All the other drivers take me." I said, knowing full well he couldn't do anything, "Why don't you get an Inwood cab to pick you up from here?" "Are you kidding on a rainy day like this?" "O.K. then I'll take you there for $18." I figured it was already $6.50 on the meter and he probably wasn't going just another few blocks. It

turns out I finally give him the ride for $14—so I take him and we're going all the hell out in East Rockaway and the meter reads something like $8.40 and he says it's just another block. At that point I went through some water, waist deep, and I let him out there. The fare was already no bargain. What did I have left for myself? He gives me $8.40 and then says "This is for yourself." I looked at it—it was a dollar bill. I said this is a 14 dollar fare. And he says, "I always come out here by cab and I always give a dollar tip. "Listen you cocksucker" I said, "It was 14 dollars." He said, "What's the matter? Can't you take it?" Then I said, "O.K. It's a deal. I'll settle, let me give you a hand with your bags." So I get out of the cab with his bags and I make like I'm satisfied with the fare. But then while I'm walking through the waist deep water I pretend I tripped and I drop his bags. He says, "Oh, my suits they're all wet." Knowing full well that it would cost him 20 bucks for the cleaning bill I said "What's the matter. Can't you take it?"

In New York the general taxi riding public has adjusted itself to the notion that if a hack actually does not perform a disservice in the line of duty, it is equivalent to performing a positive service. This gives the cabbie the upper hand that he extends through the practice of cheating.

Profiles of Cheating

Certain drivers find the established legal cost of a ride to be out of whack with their needs. Indeed, most New York hacks resort to off-the-meter negotiations and justify the need for such practices, given the working conditions of the taxi industry and the union contract. For many New York hacks, it is, "just as honest a way" to serve the public. Fleet drivers, as opposed to owner drivers, feel that they can often serve the passenger without charging excessively and also offer themselves the fleet owner's share of the income. This group of drivers will often rationalize their style of operation by reasoning with their fare that the fleet owner is certainly making an excessive profit despite the stories his accountants tell the press. If that tact doesn't win his patron over to the same moral camp, then he will proceed with a further lesson in the economics of fleet taxi operations: "Listen, you know as well as I do that even if he is losing money, it's only because he wants to protect all that other money he's got stashed away in other operations. He ain't losing money, take my word for it." No New York taxi rider who has endured the cabby's story and his pitch is going to refute him at this point in the discussion. In fact, many New Yorkers believe that the hack's economic analysis, which they hear so often, is gospel.

Super Hustler

Although there are many hacks who try to make their patrons moral accomplices to off-the-meter negotiations, many hacks are indeed not interested in explaining the beauty of sidestepping fleet owner profits. This group is the pure breed of New York hustlers oftentimes referred to as the super hustlers of the trade. They are few in number but are vast in reputation. The taxi industry as a whole continually finds its public image at the beck and call of the whims of these pirateers. Unlike the drivers who search for an all embracing economic philosophy to explain the need for their behavior, this latter group of men needs no justification. These men are the living survivors of the original undying myths of the industry. They prey upon out-of-towners and other equally unsuspecting souls who will not understand or know how to deal with the bargain he gives them. Not only do these drivers steal from the fleet owner, but they also steal from the passenger. To steal from the fleet owner is a relatively common occurrence in the New York taxi industry. A driver merely pockets the cost of the ride which he arranged off-the-meter. To fleece a passenger is to charge him a price in excess of the cost registered on the meter. Naturally it is not always easy for a passenger to know for sure if an off-the-meter price will be cheaper, the same or more expensive than one on the meter. In part, the discrepancy between the true cost of the ride and the hack's bargain price may often favor the hack rather than the passenger. Nevertheless, if the hack is a fleet driver, he automatically is making more than his share of the profits off the ride if he is able to collect anything more than half of the true cost. Thus drivers need not force an extravagant bargain upon the passenger as long as the third party, the fleet owner, is not part of the bargaining process.

The small profit secured from cheating the passenger as well as the fleet owner lures many hustlers to attempt the total hustle. Violations, such as doubling up the number of passengers travelling in his cab, asking for a flat rate, petitioning for a head charge, arranging for an out-of-town rate to the Bronx, overloading the capacity of the vehicle, and other such outright hustles characterize the super hustlers. "Charge whatever the market will bear," is in essence the working principle of this group. Beyond eliminating the union contract represented by the meter, they also in effect sabotage all official regulatory controls of the industry by charging according to the demand or need for cab service. This is the tried and true capitalist ethic at work although most taxi patrons do not recognize it as such since regulation by state and city government has become such an important part of the economic functioning of the taxi industry. A hack is no different than a small businessman at Christmas time with an array of "sale prices." They may only be sales because we as the consumer are too much in a hurry for what we demand.

New York cabbies are very well aware of when they can strike a bargain and know the passenger will have no choice in the matter. Late at night, in areas of the city where it is dangerous to be on the street, or wherever there is a sharp demand for cabs disproportionate to their availability, a hustler is king. One slick hustler indicated how much power the cab driver actually has over the public. He said:

> The best hustle I ever had was last summer. A foggy rainy night. Now at TWA there had to be 600 people, without exaggeration, all milling around trying to get out. So naturally I didn't bring my cab in. I camouflaged the cab and I walked in. Right away I got four vouchers for $15 to the city. TWA was paying their way to a hotel. Then I get the next voucher for $95. And I say "Where are you going?" Camden, New Jersey. That's a 155 dollars I got in one shot. That's knowing how to work. See? If you pull in there cold, with the light on, six snooks will jump in for this one voucher for 15 dollars. Now I got four for 60 and 95 to Camden. That's the difference in knowing what you're doin'.

> VIDICH: So what did you do? Did you put on a suit for that kind of hustle?

> EDDIE: No. I was just like I am now. The whole airport was stripped out. See. There was no cabs. This was about one in the morning and there were three cabs in the whole airport.

Beyond the proper condition for striking a bargain, the super hustler is also on the lookout for an unknowing or unsuspecting out-of-towner who wouldn't know the difference between a flat rate and a meter rate. It is this group of people who are often struck the hardest by the tactics of the hustler. An example of one super hustler's technique is enough to demonstrate their psychology:

> I am out at LaGuardia the other night and get this guy who wants to go to Newark Airport. I tell him it's a $22 trip. Okay. As soon as I get him in the cab, he passes out; he's drunk as a pig. Now LaGuardia is hot; there must be 150 people lookin' for cabs. I take the guy right around to the upper ramp and wake him up: Okay Pal! Here we are! The guy gives me $25 and gets out. I go right back downstairs and pick five guys up to New York for $4 each.

> Jesus, you are a rotten bastard.

> Listen if I don't take it, the guy is just gonna spend it over the bar; I'm doin' him a favor. This way his liver'll last longer. Ya gotta be a thief in this business.[7]

In actuality, the super hustlers are less like their normal counterparts who have a modicum of morality, because they never really settle on terms with the passenger, whereas the latter do. They demand, extort and get what they ask for. A New Yorker has no real choice in the matter as far as this group of men are concerned. There often is very little dialogue between the driver and the passenger in this situation. The driver may do no more than wrench the passenger's luggage from his hand and forcefully beckon him into his taxi. In this case the driver's economic appraisal of the passenger is more like a bandit's appraisal of the value of a bank vault. There is very little consideration among super hustlers for the opinion of the passenger.

Timid Cheaters

Although the majority of drivers shy away from outright extortion, they are usually amenable to a reasonable bargain. Their actions may very well be milder and less conniving than the super hustler of the trade; nevertheless, these "timid" drivers will cloak themselves behind the same philosophy. The *majority* of fleet drivers believe, "You've got to cheat to make a living in this business."[8] As many as 40 percent of all fleet drivers justify cheating if they are unable to make enough working strictly by the meter. Similarly 40 percent of all fleet drivers feel the inequities of the union negotiated meter split is a justification for cheating.

In fact, the most interesting conclusion of the analysis of cabbies' attitudes regarding cheating is their willingness to give as many justifications as possible for their style of life. As many as 63 percent of all fleet drivers find a personal justification for cheating among the following choices.

1. justified if the driver has a large family

2. justified if the driver cannot make enough to live by working strictly on the meter

3. justified if the meter split makes it economically impossible to make a decent day's wage

4. the practice of many drivers when fares are scarce.

Perhaps the two most important justifications are numbers two and three since they reflect most intimately upon the inequities of the industry. In this light it is significant that 57 percent of all fleet drivers listed one or the other of these reasons as justification for their approach to hacking.[9]

Although the other categories could cause corruption and extortion to develop within certain factions of the work force, these categories are more significant as irrational motivations for cheating. Thus the fact that 18 percent of all drivers justified cheating if the driver had a large family, and if the fares were scarce, says more about the driver's need to justify his actions than about the specific inequities of these situations.

Another driver opinion poll conducted by the author was concerned with drivers who blamed cheating on a select minority who practiced hustling. A total of 25 percent of all New York fleet drivers attributed the practice to a select minority.[10] Interestingly enough, 41 percent of the drivers who blamed the problem on a select minority, also went on to give personal justifications for cheating. An obvious case of popping the bag and jumping into it as well. The fleet driver, it appears, would like to deny the need for cheating, as 26 percent of all of them did. Yet he enjoys recounting his motivations for the practice and ends up standing with one foot on either side of the debate. His integrity denies the existence or extent of the problem, while his pride acknowledges the sophistication and finesse which go into making cheating necessary and possible. Indeed, if one is too honest in this business, one has no pride nor self-esteem among fellow hacks.

The degree of corruption and the justification for the need of cheating seems to vary dramatically with age. More than 55 percent of all 19 to 25 years old drivers justified cheating if the meter split makes it economically impossible to make a decent day's wage, whereas only 17 percent of all the drivers over 51 justified that choice.[11] Most notable was the fact that 50 percent of those above 51 years of age considered cheating unfounded in all cases, whereas only 12 percent of all 19 to 25 year olds gave the same opinion. It is difficult to speculate whether it is morality which grows with age or honesty which is lost through the years. However, the obvious difference between the attitudes of the younger and older drivers is an expression of the conflict between full-time and part-time drivers. The latter have no commitment to the industry and feel no threat to themselves in facing the truth. After all, the job has not become part of their lives and can easily be divorced from their own self-image. The full-timer near retirement, on the other hand, is entirely committed to his image as a hack, since his job is a mirror image of his personality. The effect is that older drivers will tend to take more pride in their work, condemming the habits of the younger hustlers. Nevertheless, some older drivers will not confess to the practice of cheating since it forces them to take a crushingly honest appraisal of their whole life at a time when men are most concerned with the worth of their lives.

With that in mind, it is quite significant that 25 percent of all the drivers over 51 years of age justified cheating if the driver could not make enough to live by working strictly on the meter.[12] This justification is somewhat more appealing to the older driver than cheating on the meter split since the latter is an affront to their union and the benefits which it offers, while the former merely finds fault with the fare rate structure and the larger economic picture of the time. In that sense the driver can feel he is simply rectifying the inequities of the recession without actually stealing from anyone in particular. If the motivation for cheating or extortion can be conceived of in terms of the larger trends of the American economy as it affects the taxi industry, then the hack's self-image will be unaffected by his actions. The sharp difference between the attitudes of the younger generation and the seasoned hacks near retirement is reflected in their divergent opinions on the culprits of extortion. Over half of all the 19 to 25 year olds consider cheating to be the practice of all drivers, whereas less than a third of all drivers over 51 feel the same way.[13] The older drivers in a sense can not categorically condemm their entire profession, in the same way as the younger generation, for that would cast doubt on the meaning of their lives. As many as 11 percent of the older drivers were willing to deny the existence of cheating entirely. This is a startling opinion coming from drivers who have long worked in an industry infested with corruption. Less than 5 percent of the younger drivers, on the other hand, were willing to deny that cheating had a place within the taxi industry.[14]

Perhaps the only opinions that the two generations share in common are the feelings that the night line drivers are more prone to extortion and hustling than the day line drivers. One out of five drivers in each group considers the night drivers most prone to cheating whereas only one out of 20 drivers in each group blames the practice on day line drivers.[15] This is not very surprising since most people know that a cab driver is less likely to cheat in broad daylight when he has less of an advantage over his patrons.

The central difference of opinion between the two groups, however, with regard to cheating is expressed in their attitude toward the part-time profession. Nearly 20 percent of the older drivers are willing to blame the part-timers for the practice of cheating whereas less than four percent of all the younger drivers blamed the part-timers.[16] The difference of opinion between the two groups points to the fundamentally different self-images of each generation. The older drivers can blame the part-timers for being the scourge of the profession and thereby protect their integrity. The younger drivers, on the contrary, can not conceive of the industry's problems as being mere reflections of their presence in the profession. They feel they are merely part-time contributors in an industry that sold out to corruption many years before they ever arrived on the scene. Nobody is willing to take the blame for cheating although many are willing to cast the first stone. Ironically, the drivers can conceptualize justifications for the corruption plaguing the hack profession yet none are willing to see themselves as the prime agents of the cheating philosophy.

The Image of the Cab Driver

To make matters worse many drivers who might not even cheat have gotten into the habit of bragging about hustling and cheating the passenger. Often times cab drivers will fabricate stories concerning how much money they've made and how they took so and so for a ride simply to impress other drivers. The practice of manufacturing wild tales and eventually disseminating them to the public has reached nearly an art form at the Bellmore cafeteria, (the principal hangout of many cabbies) on Park Avenue where any night one can sit down and hear what are purported to be stories of the greatest hustles ever told. In all fairness many drivers feel that their public image in New York is the result of the bad publicity created by drivers who tell their stories at the Bellmore cafeteria. One owner driver put it this way:

> You know who you can blame our bad image on? You can blame this on the New York Times, you can blame it on the Post, you can blame it on some of the writers that they had in the Bellmore cafeteria. Murray Kempton was the biggest fabricator in the world, what he wrote about a cab driver. These stories you hear about us are ridiculous. There's no foundation. They [journalists] come in here [The Bellmore Cafeteria]—and listen to the bullshit, pardon me, that you can edit, that goes on here. With guys blowing their own bugle so to speak which is just nonsense. You have to be able to differentiate between the truth and a fib. You know? This is a place to come and eat and relax and tell big tall stories. I'm tired of the tall tales. It's like the fisherman that went fishing. See. One guy comes in with a fish that's about a foot long and the other guy is going to tell him over a cup of coffee that he had one three feet that got away, you see.

VIDICH: Why does this happen at the Bellmore?

Ralph: I'll tell you why. There's ample parking space here. The food is good. You've got a lavatory where you can take care of personal needs, clean yourself up and sit down and eat. And everybody congregates here and the stories run wild here. One story is wilder than the other. One guy will tell you he made 50 dollars. Another guy will tell you he made 100 and another guy will tell you he went to Chicago for 500. See. Until it gets down to the last guy and he had a good week, last week. He made a thousand dollars. Now who is going to believe that. Are there enough hours in the day for a man to make that kind of money. Huh? I mean you gotta use common sense.

VIDICH: Are there any stories here that aren't fabrications?

RALPH: Very few of them. Maybe once a lifetime. And he'll tell the same story every day for the rest of his life.

VIDICH: So why do they tell these stories?

RALPH: To build themselves up. Why do you think they're telling these stories? It's nonsense. It's like a guy carrying a hundred singles in his pocket and he's got two tens on top of the singles, you see and he takes out the roll and whoever is there is looking at it sees tens. You know. He's kidding himself. That's what it is with these men. It's become like a game in here [the Bellmore]. That's all it is.

Another way that the public has gotten a bad impression of the New York cabby is due to the unbelievable and unpredictable demands that are part and parcel of driving a cab. The public learns of the cabby not only through the press but through direct contact. However, according to one driver many passengers are not aware of why a driver acts the way he does. He said:

Somebody gets into the cab that you know if you say good evening to that he won't respond. You know they hate you from before . . . from the last movie as it were. See. And then ten minutes later somebody gets into the cab and you don't say anything and they say good evening or mumble and then they will say to you, "Why are New York cab drivers so unfriendly?" I mean how are you going to cope with that. And the same thing . . . someone gets into the cab and they tell you "Gee I gotta be at 114th street in exactly 14 seconds. Can you make it from 1st street up there?" Of course personally I'm ready to fly down their throats but I go as fast as I can. The next passenger gets in and now you are barreling and they say "Driver please you're going too fast. Please slow down."

Although unfriendly cab drivers may taint the image of the profession, according to some drivers their reputation is more the result of hearing tales like the one recounted below by one disbelieving driver. He said:

How about the stories I used to hear where the drivers at 3 o'clock in the morning would get 6 Puerto Ricans right off the plane and he'd weigh 'em. . . . He'd charge them so much a pound. See? He'd charge them a dollar a pound to take them into the city. He'd put them on a toy scale and weigh the whole family right there. Can you believe a story like that?

The philosophical justifications for cheating, in one manner or another, are rampant within the industry. They might say, "How can I get that extra buck without really working for it?" Or "I'm not out here to support the boss." These attitudes stem from the fundamental economic tenet of the occupation: "In this business you've got to cheat to make a living." There are no allies under this philosophy. Fellow drivers, fleet owners, and union hierarchy represent unwanted partners in the pursuit of money.

The occupational outlook of a New York cab driver is one of the most brazen examples of unfettered entrepreneurial capitalism. A hack relies on his ability to extend his wage earning capacity beyond the borders of the law in order to survive. There is no ideological support for the moral man in the New York taxi industry.

The cause for this philosophy has grown out of the relative freedom of the driver operating his cab. The hack is accountable to no one while he is driving. Lacking the immediacy of a boss to deter his cheating, he feels quite free to entertain any bargain or operation which might make him a few dollars richer.

Owner As Fair Game

In the long history of taxi service, the taximeter has been the final judge of the price of the ride. The taximeter as it is known today had its origin at the turn of the century. The meter or clock as it is often called by hacks first came to New York in the latter part of 1907.[17] It was felt that only a meter could cure the ills of extortion then found in the city of New York. A mechanized system of determining what the passenger would pay was felt to be the solution to the problem of overcharging. Sadly enough, the men who legislated for the first taximeter did not realize that the introduction of a new contraption would never be the cure to the ills of an entire profession and their style of life. Just after the taximeter became a part of the New York scene, *Scientific American* wrote several articles on taximeter frauds. In an article in the October issue of 1911 entitled *How the driver contrives to cheat his fare,* the author states:

> On the whole . . . the most serious defect of the taximeter is the facility with which it may be employed by a dishonest driver.[18]

Ironically, the public has in a sense begun to rely on the meter as the final and only honest aspect of taxi service in New York. It is commonly felt that a meter is the only instrument that will protect the public from the avarice and pirateering of New York hacks. When in doubt about the true intentions of a New York cab driver, the passenger will often feel that the meter is his only hope of getting an honest ride. Indeed, this is true. Yet it is not as true as passengers would like to believe or as the cabby would like to have you believe. In a sense, the driver is aware of the trust value of the meter. He knows that many passengers will step out of a taxi when the driver mentions an off-the-meter negotiation. In a sense the passenger looks to the taximeter as his only true ally in the negotiation. The identification and confidence bestowed upon the taximeter by the passenger has not always been so generously given as it is today. It was not uncommon during the early years of the taximeter's history for passengers as well as drivers to doubt the reliability of the new fangled machine. Having only recently parted with the horse-drawn carriage, the taxi riding public relied upon the standard city block as the measure of the price of the ride. During these days the public was of the opinion that cabbies could operate their meters at any rate they wished. No one was sure whether the meter was working properly or whether the cabby had recalibrated it to raise his income. In addition, part of the public distrust which has so long been connected with the taximeter developed after 1913 when the city's department of licenses instituted different rate schedules; one for two passengers and the other for three passengers or more. This required a multipurpose meter capable of operating on two different rates. Naturally abuses developed whenever the driver felt he could get away with using the higher rate. To compound the problem, the 1920s witnessed the emergence of large fleets which were capable of operating large numbers of cabs at reduced prices. Police and city regulation during this time were virtually ineffective in establishing an economic standard for the taxi industry, leaving every cab the right to charge its own rate provided it was less than the ceiling price for a ride.

The evolution of distrust between the passenger and the cabby has been subtle. Where the taxi passenger at the turn of the century worried about a fast meter, the passenger of the twenties worried about getting a high priced cab. His distrust of the meter was second to his distrust of the cab driver and the ineffectual city ordinances.

With the mechanization of American industry and the increasing presence of machine made and machine operated equipment, the public began to trust what was formerly alien to their world. The public's acceptance of taximeters was a reflection of its acceptance of the machine age. The machine became an object to be trusted and relied upon rather than a weapon of crime in the hands of the driver.

Today the inevitable distrust which exists between the cab driver and his passenger remains as strong as ever. Although the public misguidedly places more faith in the accuracy of the meter than in the early days of the industry, taximeter frauds still exist. Fast meters, nevertheless, can be of no value to the fleet driver who will inevitably share his proceeds with the owner. This form of extortion is not as effective or as efficient for the seasoned hustler. In fact today only owner-driven gypsy cabs are concerned with this form of extortion.[19] The big money is made by sabotaging the meter, which thereby eliminates the fleet owner from the bargain.

The public at large may distrust a cabby, but they are usually capable of finding someone else whom they distrust a little more. This is where the sly cab driver will begin inveighing against the name of a public scapegoat or a scapegoat issue. A familiar discourse is, "I'll tell you about Lindsay and all of his liberal cronies—they can take their bleeding hearts to Nassau where they belong." What quicker way to force a friendship than to talk about common enemies or issues. This would sound like song in the ears of an Italian or an Irishman. The passenger might not need a friend like the cabby except in the context of a cab ride. For the cab driver, on the other hand, it is essential that he develop a rapport with his passenger if he wishes to keep him for a fare. In fact, the hack can not pull off his hustle unless there is some level of communication between his passenger and himself. Friendship for the driver becomes a "cover" for the deal at hand or the large tip to come.

Thus when a driver is prepared to negotiate an off-the-meter price, for the service he is to perform, he will often attempt to assuage the fear of the passenger by saying, "I'd use the meter but it ain't working" or "don't worry about the meter, you just give me what you think the ride is worth." This latter ploy appeals to the passenger. He feels he might just be able to take the cabby for a ride instead of the other way around. Having secured the interest of his patron, the driver can now proceed to the purpose at hand: driving without that ticking meter.

At one time, prior to 1968, a cabby had to do no more than gain the explicit or tacit approval of his fare to begin an off-the-meter ride. However, the practice of fleecing the fleet owner became so rampant and hurt the financial status of fleet owners to such an extent that fleet owners installed specially wired devices to curtail the ability of the driver to sidestep the meter.[20] Since 1968 a growing number of New York fleets have installed a device known as a master memory meter or passenger detection system, otherwise known as the "hot seat" to cabbies.

When a passenger sits down in the cab, the pressure of his body activates an electrical circuit connected to the meter and a delayed timer turns the meter on within 20 seconds of the moment of contact. The introduction of this mechanism has had profound effects upon the entire taxi industry. In particular, it has served to strengthen the historically long and drawn out hostility of the taxi drivers for their bosses. The fleet owner in effect is now a party to every transaction that takes place within the cab.

The hot seat is in theory the fleet owner's protection and assurance that the driver will not be able to circumvent the union contract nor attempt to bargain for the ride off-the-meter. For lack of faith in the driver's adherence to the union contract, fleet owners use the hot seat as a supplementary coercive measure to stay any non-union methods of negotiation. If the fleet owner can be assured that the meter will be used every time a passenger rides in his taxis, then he is able to reduce his overhead. In simple economics, the more paid miles registered on the meter, the more money will go to the fleet owner. When the hot seat meters were first introduced in December of 1968, the *New York Times* gave an indication of the magnitude of cheating and its consequences upon fleet operations. It stated:

> For the owners a total savings of $2.5 millon would be realized in a year if each of the 6,800 cabs brought in $1 more a day. This $1 figure is considerably lower than the first indications, although the owners will not discuss the increase.[21]

The introduction of the hot seat has revolutionized the techniques of cheating and thrown a monkey wrench into the smooth running business of corruption. In effect, the drivers feel that the hot seat is an obstacle to the proper functioning of the taxi industry.

The owner's actions appeared at first impression to be a decisive step toward breaking the rules of corruption; an impression the fleet drivers maintained in the early days of the hot seat. It took several short months before the drivers realized that the hot seat, like all machines, was capable of being sabotaged and business could proceed as usual. The fleet owners, in turn, soon realized that their attempts to upgrade the ethics of the industry by mechanical ingenuity had only created more sophisticated saboteurs.

Although the fleet owner installed more accurate and efficient electrical systems, the drivers have responded by increasing their electrical engineering expertise. In effect, the new deterrent has created a new procedure for "offing" the meter and transformed a whole system of sabotage to adjust to the latest technological developments. In many cases fleet drivers will get outside help from the neighborhood electrician or some other qualified individual willing to spend the afternoon rewiring a taxi.

The object of the latest systems of sabotage is to short circuit the hot seat device or to cut off the electrical system of the meter and overhead roof light. Some of the more prominent counter devices to the hot seat have been the giant magnet, banana plugs and false back seats, requiring short circuiting and deadening of the electrical system of the entire cab. The object is twofold: to eliminate the hot seat and to provide a "good cover" while the meter is off and the passenger is in the cab.

The most efficient counter devices to the hot seat have been those which are easily used and removed. As long as the driver can return his cab to the garage in the same electrical condition as he took it, the fleet owner has little to suspect. Ideally, then, the best sabotage is one that is not permanent. If a driver knows how to decommission the hot seat efficiently, then nobody but his fare need share his secret. Drivers of this type do not wish their secret to leak back to the fleet management or be discovered by the fleet mechanics. Recently several fleets have started a policy of checking every hot seat before it goes out for the day or night. A cabby who is tempted to cheat but does not know the subtleties of the hot seat or the meter finds himself in a quandary. If he fixes the hot seat and the fleet determines he is responsible, he is out of a job; if he becomes an honest hack, he has lost the battle to the fleet owner.

Many of New York's taxi fleets never check the hot seat or the electrical system of the cab. In garages of this kind, all that is needed are one or two skilled drivers to permanently sabotage the hot seat. Once a hot seat has been deactivated, every driver in the fleet having access to that cab enjoys the spoils. Many drivers make it their business to know just which taxis have deactivated hot seats.

Several effective measures used by New York cabbies in their effort to eliminate the hot seat depend upon ingenious gadgets. Rumors within the taxi industry hold that a few racketeering hacks are selling electromagnets to short out the meter. By attaching the electromagnet to the side of the meter, all working parts inside the meter are brought to a halt. This device has the virtue of being easily removable and requiring little technical expertise from the driver. A more sophisticated contraption known as a "banana plug" functions as an electrical resistor between the hot seat and the meter. By removing the back seat of the cab and disconnecting a few wires, the banana plug can be inserted between the meter and the pressure sensitive device in the rear seat.

Camouflage

Neither of these two devices is capable of providing a good cover. In order to tackle the separate problem of camouflage, various forms of short circuiting or rewiring are necessary. A common procedure is to break the surface of the wires leading to the identification card and crossing them. Oftentimes this short circuit alone will turn off the meter and the overhead light. A more sophisticated approach to the same problem has been to short circuit the entire electrical system through the ignition. If the cabby can hold the key slightly past the position ON and not quite as far as the position START on the key slot, this will turn off the electricity feeding the meter and the overhead light. Without a stick propped to hold the key in place, it would be somewhat tiresome and dangerous to drive with one hand on the key and one on the wheel. Those drivers using this method of camouflage usually carry a stick especially made to hold the car key in a firm position.

Last but certainly not the least interesting way to sidestep the meter is the use of false seats to cover the hot seat. As long as the bottom cushion can be thoroughly protected from the pressure of the person's weight, the hot seat will not work. In practice this involves placing a removable wooden seat cover over the length of the cushion, suspended between the two door arm rests. If the passenger is willing to prop himself against the back seat and floor without touching the bottom cushion, the driver may not even need to use a false seat. Indeed, it is not unusual for a taxi rider aware of the passenger detection system and versed in the general habits of the cab drivers to offer to sit on the floor or against the door just so that the driver can pull in the fleet owner's share of the profit.

An interesting example of the unmitigated, irrational condemnation of the hot seat and the entire taxi industry came from a young white driver. He paraphrased his feelings as follows:

> This business is for the bosses only. If I were black or Puerto Rican, I would drive a gypsy in a minute—this way everything I took in would be mine. Any black guy that works for a fleet is a sucker, anybody that buys his own cab is a sucker. The union ruined the job with the checks, hot seats, and stupid Van Arsdale. I hope and pray that every fleet in the city goes broke and out of business. These lousy owners want everything their way. Also being suspended for infractions of the rules is a farce. Every man suspended should go on Welfare then there would be no more of that.
>
> signed
> A driver that robs boss blind

The idea that anybody would attempt to thwart the smooth running of his con game was an affront to his sensibilities. The boss, police and union are just so many unnecessary obstacles in his business of hustling. This kind of undifferentiated hostility has become more prevalent since the institution of the hot seat. In a sense it has escalated the frustrations of many drivers who are not clever enough to outsmart the device. The approaches to cheating in the early days were somewhat more romantic and less intellectually demanding.

The Original Flag Up

Prior to the advent of the hot seat meters in 1968, the New York taxi fleets used flag meters. A flag attached to the side of the meter served as a lever to activate it. When the flag is in an upright position, it is visible through the front window of the cab indicating the cab is empty. Hacks refer to the various positions of the flag as if it were a clock. Indeed, the early taximeters used in America had a clock-meter combination.[23] As late as 1925 New York taxi drivers had the choice to charge by the hour or by the distance depending upon the nature of the trip. The early clock has been long gone from the industry; nevertheless, its name continues to be used to describe the modern meters.

The flag meter has four recognized positions. At 12 o'clock the flag or arm of the meter is up and the meter is not running. When the flag is up, the taxi is supposed to be vacant. When a driver gets a fare, he activates the meter by releasing the flag from the 12 o'clock position and placing it at 6 o'clock. At the end of the ride the hack places the flag at 9 o'clock to stop the meter whereupon he may return it to 12 where the meter is cleared for another trip. Perhaps the only unrecognized position is that between the hours of 1:30 and 3 o'clock on the clock. This is the position used by those drivers intent on stealing from the boss or "high flagging it" as it is known to the drivers. This position has the advantage of jamming the meter as well as providing an excellent cover for stealing from the boss. When this technique is mastered, the overhead roof light which advertises that the taxi is vacant, will be extinguished and the meter will not function. It is somewhat tricky in practice since the flag can be pushed too far activating the meter or New York's notorious pot holes might jolt the flag into the 6 o'clock position during the trip.

On a flag meter the fleet owner has no control over the acts of his drivers. The fleet owner can only expect that police surveillance will intimidate his drivers enough to thwart off-the-meter negotiations. Nowadays very few fleet owned cabs still operate with this type of meter, due to the advantages it places in the hands of the unscrupulous driver (writ large—the hack profession).

The object of the driver who is intent on making a living off the meter is to present a foolproof image of honesty to the public. The most prevalent covers used by taxi drivers driving with a flag meter are usually not quite as sophisticated as the one described above. Following, are three less effective but well used methods of riding with the flag up.

All taxis are wired so that the roof light of the taxi is extinguished when the meter is turned on. If a driver does not put the flag to 6 o'clock, he knows damn well someone might notice that his flag is up or that the roof light of the taxi is still illuminated. Naturally, many drivers not knowing about the 3 o'clock position have learned enough elementary electrical engineering to contend with the wiring system which works counter to their purposes. When the driver can rewire the taxi so that its outside lighting system contradicts the message given by the inactivated meter, he is completely safe. "Where there is a machine, there is a man to beat it," is an apt description one Puerto Rican driver gave to the task of rewiring a taxi. The challenge of the job is at this level. As a result, a great deal of the occupational skills of the trade are mere reflections of their concern with stealing from the boss.

A driver has a choice of being bold and not using any coverups at all, hoping nobody will pay attention, or protecting his hustle by employing any one of numerous covers. The easiest and perhaps the least reliable cover is the use of the off duty sign as a signal to the public that although he's vacant, he's also off duty. This procedure only works when the driver is in areas of the city not heavily patrolled by the hack police. Furthermore, it is only valid on the night shift where the cover of darkness obfuscates the real situation. This practice is by no means unusual. Since November of 1965, cab drivers have been allowed to use the off duty sign as a means to return to the garage and keep themselves from "becoming the unwilling victims of a continuous round of calls after their day or night's work."[24]

In 1964 the off-duty sign was changed from a card displayed in the front window to a permanent fixture of the overhead rooflight. This has greatly increased the driver's ability to use the off-duty sign as a "no service" advertisement any time it fits his convenience. The off-duty sign is the low trump card of the hack profession. When in doubt, a driver will automatically resort to its use. The off-duty sign is used as a general panacea for any occasion which requires a "cover." The sign nonetheless is not a very smooth way of handling an off-the-meter negotiation.

Those drivers who are more proficient with electrical wiring will short circuit the overhead rooflight whenever necessary. In this case only the passenger who has consented to an off-the-meter ride is aware of what is really happening. As a further cover many drivers will put their cap over the flag or place a portable radio in front of the meter to avoid suspicion.

Constraints On The *Laissez Faire* World Of The Cabby

All of this naturally has caused a strong fleet owner crackdown on off-the-meter negotiations. The fleet owners in New York have not merely been content to deter the drivers with hot seats. In addition to the special police force assigned to supervise the taxi industry, the fleet owners as a group have hired their own private detective agency to patrol for violations. This group, known as the "gestapo" or rat patrol to New York hacks, is only concerned with the problem of flag up violations. If the flag is up or the meter is not being used, the gestapo is empowered to issue a summons for the driver to appear before a hack court. This hired police force serves the following threat to drivers, "If you don't produce good bookings, we'll catch you sooner or later even if the hot seat doesn't." Many of New York's fleet still have some flag meters in use. Flag meters unlike button meters with the accessory hot seat device afford the fleet owner little protection. The hot seat, on the other hand, has had some success in reducing easy steals, but has had unfortunate side effects on the stability of the fleet work force. Many drivers have migrated to garages with flag meters feeling that the hot seat, gestapo surveillance, and fleet owner production quotas have made the job too difficult to be worth its while.

Unlike any other single profession, New York hacks have more regulatory bodies, enforcement agencies, private espionage outfits and citizens keeping a watch over their actions than any other profession of equal status and rank.[25]

How the Mice Play

In order to deal with the police, gestapo, Port Authority police, and an array of other agencies, the New York cabby has to know as much about their surveillance habits as these cops know about his habits. The owner driver and the fleet driver learn through close contact day in and day out the major areas patrolled by each police force. The simple idea is to develop a complete knowledge of where not to go while cheating. Like the screen system, the driver can never be 100 percent sure that he will avoid getting caught if he abides by his knowledge of police surveillance patterns. The various police agencies are by no means totally predictable although there are certain locations and areas in New York where they can be expected to be at all times.

Taxi drivers have developed a very sophisticated game of evasion from the cops on patrol. Police surveillance has never been very effective. Sources working within the old hack bureau under the supervision of the New York Police Department claimed less than one out of every 100 drivers violating the rules governing drivers of public hacks is ever apprehended.[26] The police department can not afford the financial investment of excessive surveillance of the taxi industry. As a result, the hack police have had to create a feeling among taxi drivers of the omnipresence of law enforcement agents.[27] Despite the desire of the hack police to convey a feeling of omnipresence to the taxi driver, their rhetoric is more of a police ideology than a reality. For the most part, this ideology represents a convenient evasion of the need for better surveillance of the entire city. One reason for the ineffective police supervision of the taxi industry rests with the cab driver himself. The driver in effect can play a game of cat and mouse with the hack police because police surveillance is only able to cover those areas of the city which will yield the highest number of summonses on a per hour basis. Due to police assignments in areas of concentration of violations, drivers can avoid summonses by avoiding those areas of the city in which the hack police are known to patrol most frequently.[28] The most obvious hangouts of the police are at all major transportation terminals leading into and out of the city. In addition, it is not uncommon for the police to pay special attention to the bridges and tunnels leading to the outer boroughs of Manhattan.

Transportation terminals are major breeding grounds for violations. The greatest opportunities and the greatest business is usually connected with terminals such as Grand Central Station, the East Side airline terminals, Port Authority Bus Terminal, and the two New York airports. Not only are these the most profitable sources of fares, they also offer the greatest opportunity for the driver to cheat. The police are well aware of this situation. The greatest number of police employed by the city or private agencies are found around these terminals. Although the driver is aware of this phenomenon, it is by no means a positive deterrent to his continued hustling at these areas. For the determined hustler, there are only two possibilities. Either he becomes a recognized face to the hack police and loses the power of anonymity, or he learns to avoid direct contact with hack police while passing anywhere near their sectors of patrol. The super-hustlers of the profession generally tend to be well known and much discussed by the hack police.[29] They, as a rule, must be extremely careful if they wish to continue outright extortion. A single misjudgment of a situation and their driving days may be numbered.

Cheating is the driver's sublimated way of expressing his hostility and resentment against the conditions of economic repression. In a sense it is an alternative to collective bargaining within the industry although it can never replace the legal value of a sound contract. One fleet driver, representing the views of many others claimed, "They (the boss) force you into a situation where you have to steal to make ends meet."[30] In this sense the cheater is performing a rational act aimed at remedying the uncertainties of his occupation.

Ironically though, the existence of cheating favors the bosses if cheating is viewed as an alternative to collective bargaining. Though the driver may be totally successful in his efforts to increase his income, his actions are formulated outside the framework of the law and depend upon the defensive tools of sabotage, as expressed in his practice of short circuiting the hot seat (and the owner's share of the money) and coercion as expressed in his relationship with the passenger.

It is not suprising that the fleet owners have allowed cheating to continue, since it indicates that collective bargaining can be undermined by giving the driver the immediate pleasure of stealing some of his money. In fact, fleet owners have gone so far as acknowledging the existence and need for cheating within the industry. As one fleet spokesman stated in 1971, "hustlers are present in the industry and they have to engage in such practices to make a living."[31] The owner's acceptance of the problem of cheating reflects his willingness to let the driver steal a crumb while the major profits are siphoned into his own pockets. The owner's use of hot seats, police enforcement and production quotas has not been effective but it has placed the driver in a precarious position while making a living. This problem has worked against the best interests of the public since drivers are more concerned with making a living than with serving those in need of their services.

2

Beating The Hack's System

The Public's Response

Is the passenger really at the mercy of the New York hack? Not quite as much as the cabby would like you to think. For every system of defense the cabby uses against his potential passenger, there exist standard and well-used systems of offense. The question is how do you catch a cab? For many people, this is of no interest and perhaps will never concern them. Nevertheless, there are many people in the city who suffer at the whims of the hack through no personal fault of their own. This latter group of people have developed customs for hailing and procedures for locating the nearest available cab.

Like a hitch hiker, you, a taxi rider are asking a ride from a man who is not altogether sure of your good intentions. You must prove to him that not only do you appear to be a respectable man or woman, but that you have all the intentions in the world of paying him his fare. Hailing a cab is normally a fairly simple procedure, if the passenger can gain the driver's attention. To hail a cab on a busy night on a midtown street may not be quite as easy. Although drivers pride themselves on their peripheral vision, they are not always able to detect somebody hailing them off the curb. On deserted streets no tricks are needed to attract a cab. On a busy, heavily crowded street, it is just the opposite. Potential taxi riders will go as far as blocking a lane of traffic to catch the attention of a cabby driving down the far side of the avenue. Often enough, passengers realize that catching a cab necessitates standing on the right side of the street. Cab drivers generally are attracted by activities which they feel will produce taxi patrons. Hailing a cab from the vicinity of these spots usually makes the problem much simpler. The signs most often used when hailing a cab are the "high hand," "the beckoning hand," a doorman's whistle, or one's own whistle. These signs provide the initial call but are by no means the only forces at work when a cabby catches your plea for service. If you can't sell yourself and your surroundings, the cab driver may very well ignore your hail. This specific problem is indigenous to the ghettoes and outer boroughs of New York. In these areas the cab driver's discrimination is felt the most. As a result, the people who often can least afford taxis are often the most discriminated against. A good hail is of no value to you if the cabby doesn't like where you live or who you are.

Nobody is going to change his address and his appearance just to hail a cab. It just is not quite that important to ride by taxi. Nevertheless, there are certain things that you can do to grab a cab even if you look entirely unacceptable to the hack and are going just where he intends to avoid travelling. Although you may not be able to stop a cab, the synchronized light system often will. All you have to do is patiently stand on a street corner near enough to a well used taxi corridor and wait for a taxi to get caught by the light. This often can be arranged by crossing the street so that the driver does not have a chance to run the light. Usually though it is better to sneak up behind the cab out of view of the driver's side view mirror. If the doors are locked, only one other trick will get you inside the cab. If the driver deems your appearance to be acceptable, you calmly explain to him that you are going to midtown Manhattan or any area in which he seems bent on going. If you are one of the lucky ones, he'll open the door and take you. At this point the driver will say, "Where did you say you were going" just to banish his worst suspicions. At this point, either you are telling the truth and all is well, or he sees you've just pulled a fast one on him and he'll say, "Sorry, buddy, I don't go there and I wouldn't go even if you showed me how." There is only one response to that; "I've got your hack number and medallion number on this piece of paper and so help me, if you give me any trouble, I'll report you." If the impasse gets any worse, there are two alternatives. If you've got the time, you can wait it out on the back seat, assured that the partition and locked doors will protect you from the cabby.

The other choice, and perhaps the most popular initial choice of all New York's outer borough taxi patrons, is to hail a gypsy cab. More than likely if you are standing in a place where a taxi will refuse you, a gypsy will be nearby to serve you.

Cruising Patterns

If, indeed, you are strictly a taxi patron and find gypsy cabs to be either a risk or insufficient in number to replace taxi service, where then do you find a taxi? New York cab drivers have preestablished cruising patterns throughout the city. As noted earlier, the driver is concerned with maximizing his certainty of locating a fare. In the outer boroughs the problem is compounded. Not only are there normally few fares to entice the driver to pass through the area, but drivers have heavier competition from the gypsy cab trade. In part, the taxi driver will pick streets which he knows produce fares but he will also cruise streets whose residents patronize taxis. In the outer boroughs of New York, the latter possibility is becoming increasingly rare with the advent of the gypsy.

Major throughways accessible to the pedestrian and punctuated by red lights often are the best places to snatch a taxi. Most taxis keep to the main streets in part because they expect their passengers to look for them on the main streets. The driver's and passenger's shared knowledge of where to find each other represents what little service characteristics exist in the taxi industry. In the area of midtown Manhattan, a driver's job of locating a fare is fairly easy if he can beat his competition. A passenger in this same area has no problems of any kind. Nonetheless when the scenery changes and the driver and passenger are both in the Bronx, the certainty of finding each other is replaced with conjecture. "Where would a cab be at this time of day" is reciprocated by the driver's query, "On which one of these streets will I find a fare?" In part, the driver and the passenger respond to the problem at hand by scouting out their rivals. If a couple of people down the street also appear to be beckoning for a cab, the passenger might feel that the street just isn't big enough for two. What then? He might very well walk over to the other side of the street if it is two way or pick a parallel street nearby.

The driver may find himself in similar straits with gypsy or taxicab competition. Unlike the courtesy among passengers hailing cabs, there is no love between cab men. Although one driver may have the edge on getting a fare, often as not he will race his opponent to get ahead and nose him out of the picture. If this procedure proves unsuccessful and his adversary can maintain the lead on his cab, the driver will either slow down and look for stray fares if he thinks he is on a good street, or he will circle back in the other direction from which he came. If indeed there is a good street nearby, the cabby might try it, hoping there is less competition there. This chance is only taken if the driver is familiar with the alternative route and knows it to be a good bet.

The areas in which cruising patterns become an integral part of the service provided by taxis are the Bronx, Brooklyn, Queens, and scattered areas in northern Manhattan. In these areas of the city, the passenger has difficulty catching a cab unless he is familiar with the cruising habits of hacks. The major arteries serving as "semi fixed routes" for taxi service vary with the time of day and the level of competition from gypsy cabs and other yellow taxis. In the Bronx, the Grand Concourse, Bruckner Boulevard, 161st Street, 149th Street, Tremont Avenue, Westchester Avenue, and Southern Boulevard are the major routes upon which the driver and the passenger can expect to meet with the most certainty. The South Bronx in general is a better area to locate a taxi than the less populated northern and eastern fringes of the borough. The South Bronx is the proper area to find a cab, only because of its proximity to the bridges leading to Manahattan. As such, the above named thoroughfares become important as feeders to funnel the taxi driver over the bridges leading to Manhattan. Taxi patrons know that their effort to secure a taxi on these streets is aided by standing on the proper side of the street. If a cab driver sees the person pointed in the proper direction, he is more than likely to stop without hesitation. The number of routes tends to diminish with the lessening demand for cabs, from a maximum of ten in the daytime to no more than three or four at night. The Grand Concourse, 161st Street and 149th Street become the only sure bets after six o'clock in the evening. The shared knowledge of the semifixed routes used by taxis is the only effective way taxi patrons are able to contend with the sparse service offered in the Bronx.

Similarly, Brooklyn and Queens have preestablished taxi corridors. In these boroughs, unlike the Bronx, the semifixed routes are somewhat more comprehensive of their entire geography. This is a result of the fact that the two New York airports attract taxis. These boroughs, as a result, have longer and more developed semifixed routes; not only can a driver return to Manhattan, but if he happens to be taken to a location near a New York airport, he may go to the airport instead. The two major fixed routes in Brooklyn and Queens are Flatbush Avenue and Queens Boulevard. A person living in the vicinity of either one of these thoroughfares is assured that he will be able to catch a taxi at any time of day. During the night time, Queens Boulevard tends to serve Queens somewhat more satisfactorily than Flatbush Avenue serves Brooklyn. In the daytime, though, the situation is reversed.

Queens Boulevard is the Queens taxi artery. The driver knows he can use it instead of the Long Island Expressway en route to Kennedy Airport. Access to the airport and the city allows Queens Boulevard to be used as a fixed source of cabs. Other important, but less fixed, cruising routes used by taxis in Queens are Junction Boulevard, Northern Boulevard, 21st Street and Roosevelt Avenue. These routes are dependable for taxi service because they serve as connecting arteries to midtown Manhattan and LaGuardia Airport. The taxicab driver in New York has developed these apparently semifixed routes in order to accurately locate as much business as easily as possible. One veteran cab driver explained the cruising system in the following way:

Now they [the outer borough residents] yelled they weren't getting service. How many cabs are supposed to be in any given area to service x amount of people? You know it's a funny thing when it comes to a cab, you walk out of a house and you want a cab at the snap of a finger. But you walk over to a busstop or a subway and you're willing to wait twenty minutes, thirty minutes and you don't say a word. But when it comes to a cab you yell your head off because the cab isn't there. But the thing is the cabs can't be all over. And then the cabbie is just like any other business. The cabbie is always going to be in areas where they know they can make a living. Why should I go ahead and ride around like in certain parts of Brooklyn like Canarsie? You understand? And at certain hours of the day. It's crazy, you understand. Say it's 12 o'clock at night. I'm going to ride around Canarsie? People are home in the house sleeping. But I know the people in Manhattan or let's say Flatbush Avenue in Brooklyn are going to be coming out of bars or coming out of the theater or they maybe need a cab. I'm going to be there.

No doubt there are other inequities in the actual operation of the cruising system throughout the city. Many potentially worthy areas and streets are avoided through a driver's lack of knowledge of the entire city or fear of being robbed in a black community.

Brooklyn without a doubt is underserved. There are far fewer semifixed routes in this borough than all the others. In part, this situation is an outgrowth of the problems of gypsy competition and the fear of being robbed in areas having a history of such occurrences. Besides Flatbush Avenue there are precious few routes on which taxis can be found at any time of day. Atlantic Avenue, Fulton Street, Broadway, 9th Street, and the downtown Brooklyn business district during the day are the only other substantial taxi corridors. On these corridors drivers are often more discerning of your appearance and final destination than in Queens. In Brooklyn it is much more important to be headed in the proper direction than in any of the other boroughs. Even the ruse of heading toward Manhattan does not always work in Brooklyn. Taxis returning to Manhattan over the Williamsburg Bridge will often pass by as many as four or five separate parties supposedly headed toward the city. The cabby knows all the tricks passengers use. He will even go as far as distrusting the supposedly safe bet to Manhattan. A person might very well be standing right in the entrance ramp to the Williamsburg Bridge and the cabby will still refuse to take him over the bridge. Although this behavior is the exception rather than the rule, it clarifies the psychology of the driver. To be destined for the same area the driver is headed is an essential part of the success formula for hailing a cab.

Hack Stands

Above and beyond the service offered by fixed routes the city of New York has a limited number of hack stands at major activity centers, hotels, terminals, restaurants, and at Kennedy and LaGuardia airports. The hack stand serves to supplement the semifixed cruising routes by providing a waiting place for vacant taxis. Instead of the driver coming to the passenger, the hack stand allows the passenger to come to the driver. As a result, hack stands are rarely located in little used areas of the city or in the low density areas in outer boroughs. For the most part working hack stands are indigenous to Manhattan and the two New York airports. Drivers will only use a hack stand if they know the nearby area will produce a sufficient number of passengers to warrant waiting. In Manhattan, hack stands will not necessarily help passengers locate service, although they will provide a measure of protection from speeding taxis. For the driver, on the other hand, a hack stand functions like a semifixed route does in areas outside of Manhattan. As in the case of semifixed routes, the hack stand guarantees to the driver a greater chance of finding a fare. Amidst the competition and oversupply of taxis in the midtown area, the hack stand allows the cabby certain fixed spots where he can be certain of a fare. This is of critical importance in the midtown area since over half of all the vehicles on the streets are taxis and as many as half of them are empty—cruising for fares.

With the exception of the transportation terminals, New Yorkers using hack stands usually are patrons of expensive restaurants or hotels. This class of people rarely has to prove itself to the taxi driver. These passengers can be certain that any driver parked in a hack stand will take them where they want to go. If there is a problem, the doorman or dispatcher, where available, provides a visible deterrent to any driver's intent on screening the passenger.

Traffic on Fifth Avenue, above, 1929. (World Wide Photos) Below, 1974. (Photography by Paul Vidich)

Knowing how to beat the hack at his own game is especially valuable at Kennedy and LaGuardia Airports. The airline terminals, with exceptions, have self-service taxi stands. For lack of a dispatcher, passengers are often able to pick and choose the taxi they want although the cabby is also able to reciprocate the gesture. Some of the worst violations and extortionist activities take place at the two New York airports. The hustling hack or airport rat, as he is called, has two goals: to avoid going anywhere except Manhattan and to make as much money as possible off one long haul to the city. The problem at the airport is not finding a cab or worrying about whether the driver likes your appearance, but finding an honest hack willing to take you where you want to go. The cabby has a disadvantage in a hack stand in so far as he is unable to monopolize his services. If he refuses to serve you, there are always more taxis available. However the passenger is not totally safe from the clutches of the cab driver. Certain brazen cabbies will actually get out of their cabs and choose the passengers they wish to pick up. One driver explained how he conned passengers into his cab in this way:

I worked the airports religiously everyday. I would park in the parking lot, dress up and go into the Overseas terminal, and I used to hustle. The live ones, you know. No New York. Just the out of town stuff.

VIDICH: How does that work?

AL: Oh that works fantastic. Every night I used to go out of town. And I would dress up with a suit. I had a regular attache case and I had my car parked in the parking lot. I had to walk in there and I used to screen the work.

VIDICH: You'd screen the people you wanted to pick up? So how did you do it?

AL: By where they're going and then we'd make a deal. And I had a place to pick them up.

Although the passenger may not have a problem securing a taxi, he may very well have difficulty with the cabby's version of the price of the ride. The airport traveller is the tired and unsuspecting passenger par excellence. For lack of knowledge of New York taxi rates and the general character of the taxi profession, airport passengers are the worst suckers for the hustles of airport rats. An off-the-meter deal from a New York airport is nearly always stacked against the passenger.

This is by no means a small problem at New York's airports since more than 22 million people fly in and out of New York each year and as many as 40 percent of them rely on the taxi driver to supply their transportation needs.[1]

Public Recourse: The Hack Trial

For those passengers who have serious complaints against the extortions of cabmen there exists a complaint procedure, maintained by the City of New York, that allows the passenger an opportunity to see justice done. However, most passengers victimized by the cab driver rarely take the opportunity to bring the cab driver to trial. Less than 7 percent of all taxi users who have been victimized by unscrupulous cab drivers are willing to report their complaint.[2] This breakdown in the public's concern over the actions of cab drivers is largely due to the inconvenience involved in filing a complaint and the consumer's unwillingness to waste his time over what most regard as a temporary nuisance. The end result of this situation is that out-of-towners are victimized more than any other group since they are thoroughly unfamiliar with the legal means of retaliation and rarely have the time to wait for the complaint to reach the hearing. Like the inefficient and unorganized court system of our country, the complaint procedure against New York cabbies offers no quick trial. As the Taxi and Limousine Commission reported:

> Outmoded and inefficient procedures caused hearings to be scheduled months after the date of the filing of the complaint, even in cases that required little or no investigation.[3]

This situation usually leads the irritated passenger to forget the misdemeanors of his driver and cast his problem off to bad luck or any other explanation that allows him to quickly cast aside the petty annoyance of a cab driver.

The Cabbies' Defense: Sabotage and Municipal Apathy

Prior to the creation of the Taxi and Limousine Commission in 1971 there was little hope to be placed in the legal procedures of the old Hack Bureau's trial system since over one third of all scheduled hearings never took place. Since 1971 the Taxi and Limousine Commission has tried to improve the hack trial by encouraging the public to voice their complaints to the Commission. However the Commission has not been too successful in improving the system. Either the case is dismissed because the passenger, in his rage to prosecute, forgot to get the proper information to identify the guilty driver or the driver manages to delay the proceedings until the passenger is thoroughly exasperated and decides to forget the matter. The cab driver usually accomplishes this goal by not showing up at the hearing. This procedure wears down the stamina of the complainant and allows the driver to get off on a suspended sentence.

As many as 30 percent of all hearings end up in a suspended sentence due to the absence of the driver.[4] This problem is a major one since it completely sabotages the due process of law and denies the consumer any legal retaliation.

For those who actually get the driver to trial, less than one-third are able to reprimand the driver.[5] The hack bureau and its successor, the Taxi and Limousine Commission, have been notoriously lenient on cabbies. As proof of this one cab driver noted, "I know guys who got caught 30 or 40 times doing arm jobs and never got more than a day off." Prior to 1972, those drivers who did get punished, generally received one to two day suspensions for their infractions which supposedly forced the driver to stop working for the length of the suspension. However, most drivers merely rescheduled their work week to compensate for the two day vacation and were never affected by the punishment. Now, however, the Taxi Commission fines the drivers as well as temporarily suspending their license. According to one cabby the fines have cut down the number and type of arm jobs being done since, "If they catch you it's a $25 fine and a ten suspension. So to steal 50 cents doesn't make sense anymore. I don't ride the arm in Manhattan. Only out of town. And what are you stealing? For 50 cents you're taking this risk of $25 and 10 days. It doesn't make any sense."

The leniency of the old hack bureau operated by the police department was often encouraged through union pressure. In fact Van Arsdale still maintains several men at all hearings to reduce the sentences of its members. The obvious strength of Van Arsdale and the leniency of the police department is clearly seen in the consumer hearings of 1970. Of the 1,430 hearings scheduled, not one passenger was able to revoke the license of a cab driver.[6] This state of affairs was not indicative of any improvement in the general lot of cab drivers, but was a failure of municipal government to protect the rights of consumers. This was confirmed by the 1971 Taxi and Limousine Commission studies of the Police Department's Hack Bureau:

> Given the schedule of penalties prior to Local Law 12, even the worst violators continued hacking since it took 10 convictions of major violations within 18 months to get one's license revoked, an almost impossible feat.[7]

Generally, drivers have been able to get away with anything they want since few passengers complain, and those who do rarely get a hearing and those who get a hearing rarely are able to reprimand the driver. Under this system of justice, the driver can easily ignore the threats of the patron who is indignant over his actions. One hustler with a great deal of courtroom experience gave a clear example of the frustration many people undergo when trying to prosecute New York cab drivers. He related it to the author in the following conversation:

HARRY: There are a lot of things you're not supposed to do, my friend, in this world, but you gotta do. Ha ha ha. It's very good for the guy that sits up on the twenty first floor of the Taxi Commission and says you must do this and this. He's not affected by anything.

VIDICH: Have you had any run ins with them?

HARRY: Oh a few yea.

VIDICH: What happens?

HARRY: I usually beat 'em.

VIDICH: Give me an example of what happens when you go down for a hearing.

HARRY: I beat the number two man in the board of education on a refusal.

VIDICH: Really? What was the case?

HARRY: Ha ha ha. The case was there were four of us parked at this terminal and the flight came in and we were all hustling, as you say, you know up and down, nobody near the cabs. Ha ha ha ha. So a couple of days later I get a notice in the mail that at such and such a night at such and such a terminal at Kennedy you refused this party. Well generally if I have a beef with somebody I write it down in a little book so that if something comes in the mail months later I can refer back and it will come to me. Nothing came to me about this particular thing. So I went down there [for the hearing] and the party wasn't there. But I got the complainants name off the board. It sounded like a man and I did have a beef with a man that particular night. In fact he was taking numbers [of the taxicab] and everything. So anyway the guy don't show up. So the hearing officer says its dismissed without prejudice, which means he [the complainant] can reopen it in four months but I got nothing to say about it. Sure enough three months later I get another letter. I go down there and I walk into this room and there's a guy with his back to me and he's got an attache case with all papers and everything and he's having a fight with the hearing officer. And the first words I hear are "This is the most inept operation in the whole country" he says, "I'll take that back, the whole world. Nobody operates like this Taxi Commission." So right away I know this guy is in my corner, the hearing officer, see. It seems when we were supposed to go down there the first time I went down, they sent him the letter for the wrong day the next day. Ha ha ha. So when he went down I wasn't there. That's what he was burned up about.

VIDICH: And this was the guy who was making the complaint?

HARRY: Yea.

VIDICH: So then what happened?

HARRY: So here's what happened. He starts in with this story, on such and such a night at this particular terminal he and his wife came out and they asked the cab drivers to take them to Kew Gardens or something. And they all ran away. So right away I knew what happened. He was so mad at these guys going through the terminal and turning him down that he took the numbers of the cabs parked at the curb where there were no drivers and no lights on. That's what he did. Right away I knew. I didn't say nothing yet, it wasn't my turn. So then I interrupted the hearing officer and I said, "Can I ask this gentleman a question? Do you recognize me?" He said, "I don't recognize any of them. They all had their windows closed." I said, "Well how did they know you were going to Flushing?" or wherever the hell he was going. The hearing officer said, "Yea, that's a good question. Answer that." He couldn't answer it and he was getting red up to here. Strike one for me. Ha ha ha. So then they're battling back and forth and the two guys again and he looks at my trip card and I was nowhere near Kennedy airport at the time this happened. I had Bayridge or something, ha ha, down there. "Well this man was in Bayridge Brooklyn at the time you says you got his number. I can't convict him on this flimsy testimony of yours" he's telling him. He's giving him this English, see. "Dismissed." Now a friend of mine who was also on the same line he's in the [hearing] waiting room. He's next. Now I'm convinced that's what happened. He took the names and numbers of the four cabs at the curb because everybody else refused him that he talked to. So they threw him out too. Because he was nowhere near this place at this time. So that was one little guy who fought back against the establishment.

VIDICH: And he lost?

HARRY: And he lost all four guys. Ha ha ha. He was so mad I thought he was going to have a heart attack. He figured he was such a big shot that he was going to nail four little cab drivers and we turned the tables on him. He went out of there with his tail between his legs. I bet he never goes back to the Taxi Commission again.

VIDICH: Do you think the Commission is any better than the Hack Bureau?

HARRY: Oh I think so. Yea. These guys have a little bit of mercy, not much but a little bit. Where the old Hack Bureau, they were cops and they couldn't care less, they just as soon lock you up as not—some of them.

VIDICH: They'd throw you in?

HARRY: Yea, they'd lock you right up if you gave them any lip. These guys you can give lip to easily. They're pretty decent. At least one of them is anyway.

The consumer is at the driver's mercy and there is precious little to be done about his plight. The aggravations and wasted time of complaining against a driver often span several months of waiting for the trial to take place, a trial that is by no means certain of taking place nor likely of reaching any form of punishment, as the above example indicates This situation allows the driver to operate without any legal restrictions upon his behavior.

Broadcasting System

Fleet owners justifiably contend that the negative image the public has of the taxi industry is a consequence of their employees. One fleet owner flatly stated that the reason the public had such a low opinion of the taxi owners is that, "the irate driver serves as a broadcasting system to the public and any time a driver has a gripe against the fleet owner, he will go out and tell the world about it." The fleet owner feels that his image is bandied about by drivers with something on their mind who are unwilling to fight it out directly with the boss. This contention is undoubtedly true, though one must hasten to explain that an entire city can not develop a portrait of a fleet owner from the publicly broadcast gripes of a few men.

True to political form, the owners blame their own low credibility on the machinations of a few extremely talkative men. They insist that public thoughts of mafia intrigue, public swindle, and rejuggling accounting figures are just a reflection of the mentality of the New York hack and no reflection upon themselves. As one owner said, "Don't you think it is logical that a driver who has cheated me all his life is going to expect that I'm doing the same to him?" In placing the responsibility for the taxi industry's bad image upon the driver, the fleet owner denies his own guilt.

The fleet owner would like the public to believe he is a hard working business man with not much profit, if any at all, to show for all his investments. The driver undoubtedly sees a little bit of himself in the fleet owner and takes exception to the owner's inflated self descriptions. As a result of the fleet owner's numerical inferiority to their employees, the owners have spent considerable amounts of money safeguarding their image. A trade paper, The Taxi News, devotes itself to glorifying the goodness and sincere best wishes of the fleet owners in working to better their drivers' conditions. The paper is a free publication to the driver made available by the generosity of fleet owners. The owners realize that the greatest threat to their public image lies with possible discontent amongst the ranks of their own drivers. The owner cannot attack or ferret out the most dissident hacks since he is faced with the power and support each driver gains through his association with the taxicab union. Instead of expedient action, the owners must face the effects of possible reprisals for attempting to exorcize drivers who are a threat to their public image. Historically, before the advent of the present union, owners would not bother to worry about the recriminations of other drivers if they felt it necessary to fire certain troublemakers. The old days of the industry were quite good for the owner. At that time drivers were divided from each other by company and had virtually no power whatsoever to confront their boss. If an owner fired a driver, there was no union to take exception with his actions.

The present hostility and resentment generated against the fleet owner is intimately related to the early development of New York's taxi industry. The early structure and operations of the major taxi fleets determined the quality of service provided to the public. Although the public has reserved its condemnations of the taxi industry to the cab driver, the fundamental causes of the driver's actions are to be found in the manner in which the industry has been controlled and operated by the fleet owners.

The problems plaguing the public today are no different from those in the past. The public in New York has never been served properly by the taxi industry. This is a situation that has existed in New York since the earliest days of taxi service.

3

Organization Of The Taxi Industry

An Historic Overview

Development Of The Taxi As Public Transportation

The electric hansom cab was the first public automobile to serve the city of New York. Under the Electric Carriage and Wagon Company 12 hansom cabs were placed on the streets of New York in July of 1897.[1] This was the first commercial use of the automobile in America. These horseless carriages, as they were then called, were remarkably similar to the horse drawn cabs of the day. The designers had felt that an unobtrusive vehicle would be received more easily than one that departed wildly from the character and design of the existing horse drawn cabs—a decision which led to the early public acceptance of electrical hansoms. The *Scientific American* of March 1899 noted: "The success of the electric cab on the streets of our city is one of the most significant facts in matters of city transportation."[2]

The electric cab had an early advantage over the gasoline operated vehicle, among the wealthy consumers, since it was odorless and virtually silent. In contrast, the gasoline engine was extremely distasteful to the automobile buying public. In describing the electric cabs *Scientific American* of March 13, 1897 noted its virtues over that of the gasoline powered automobile: "The motion of the cabs is pleasant in the extreme. There is no vibration such as is often found in carriages driven by one of the petroleum products."[3]

Electric cabs were relatively cheap compared to the hansom cabs of the day. This was made possible by the cost efficiency of operating an electric cab which was said to be over ten times cheaper than a horse and buggy operation.[4] However, the Electric Vehicle Company was not able to reduce its rates to reflect the cost efficiency of the electric cabs since station operations required hundreds of men for tending the electric cabs and their batteries. As a result, labor costs and overhead ate up the cost efficiency of the electrically driven motor cabs.

Despite sizable problems, the Electric Vehicle Company expanded its New York fleet to 62 in 1898 and then to 100 in 1899.[5] Moreover the same company became a holding unit for operating automobile fleets in major cities. Subsidiaries were established in Chicago, New York, Boston and Philadelphia and an effort was made to expand operations into 16 states. Financial trouble soon developed for the Company in 1900. They had predicted manufacturing 8,000 cabs in 1900 but soon cut that figure to 2,000 and reduced the labor force in their Hartford automobile factory. *The Horseless Age* declared: "Where thousands of Lead Cabs were to be found in service we find but fifty, groaning around with every sign of wear and tear, half the time in the hospital and indifferently patronized at that."[6]

There were other reasons the Electric vehicle didn't succeed. As most people realized during that epoch there were a few things wrong with the vehicle. The battery weighed 1,200 pounds which was almost half of the total electric cab load of 2,500 pounds. Moreover, the one and one half Lundell type motor could only achieve a maximum of 15 miles per hour and was limited to a radius of 25 miles on a recharged battery. Recharging batteries took eight hours and changing a battery was even worse. This required an overhead crane to haul out the old battery and a sizable plant to house the machinery.

The Electric Carriage and Wagon Company folded in January of 1907 when 300 of the company's 750 cabs were burned in a garage fire.[7] This event accelerated the emergence of the gasoline powered automobile and gave the automobile manufacturers an undisputed monopoly over the sale of public cabs in New York City. Within nine months of the disastrous fire, the gasoline powered vehicle took over the role of public transportation.

The taxi industry as we know it today began with the introduction of the first gas powered automotive metered taxis into New York on October 1, 1907.[8] They were introduced without much notice from the press for no one could envision the revolutionary consequences the automotive taxi would have on urban transportation. In fact, the very word taxi was introduced into America on this occasion to describe the automotive vehicle for hire. The word was derived from the French word taxi-metre or tax registered by the meter for the price of the ride, but was abbreviated to taxi and became a synonym for the automobile providing the service.

Electric hansom cabs were introduced into New York City in 1897. (Museum of the City of New York)

A man named Harry Allen was the first to introduce the automotive taxi to New York.[9] Furthermore, his operation was relatively large compared to those of the horse drawn carriages since he began with a fleet of 50 French Darracq taxis. The New Taxicab Company, as it was appropriately called, was a first step toward the mass production of urban transportation service. The taxi had the advantages of speed and efficiency over the horse and buggy operation, not to mention that it was cheaper to operate a motor driven taxi than it was to operate a horse and buggy. As a result, the initial rates charged by the Darracq taxis were appreciably cheaper than horse drawn cabs could possibly offer.

The old hansom cabs were primarily for the rich and leisured classes of New York. These two young women walking down Park Avenue were the standard fare for the 19th century cab driver. (Photograph by Byron, The Byron Collection, Museum of the City of New York)

The cab driver of today operates much the same as he did 100 years ago—including hustling fares at the entrances of the city, expecting a big tip, parking his cab in the middle of the street and posing for pictures in front of Brentano's Bookstore. (Top, The Staten Island Historical Society; bottom, Paul Vidich)

Soon after 1907 the horse and the automotive taxi parted company and developed separate markets within the city. The horse drawn buggy had primarily served the wealthy upper class and tourists visiting the city. With the competition of the taxi, it became apparent that the horse was losing its monopoly over luxury service.[3] Nevertheless, the taxi was also expanding and developing new demands for personalized vehicular transportation within economic and social classes which had previously never relied on the horse and buggy. Many people were quickly won over to the taxi as a cheap and competitive substitute for the subway and trolleys which had not yet

In 1907 the first taxicab was introduced into America on the streets of New York. It was called a taxi because of the presence of a taximeter (French for a meter registering the tax on the ride) on the side of the cab. (The Staten Island Historical Society)

been fully developed. As a result of the new demand for taxi service, the automobile and the horse drawn buggy were able to coexist. In effect, the markets of the two became segmented quite rapidly and have since developed along entirely different lines.[4]

The early years of the industry were primarily controlled by large fleet operations. In fact, fleet operators were able to monopolize the services provided in these days because of the concessions they were able to obtain from terminals, piers, railroad stations, hotels and restaurants which were the primary source of business for the taxi industry.

Prior to 1913 the taxi industry was not legally regarded as vested with public interest.[5] The major taxi fleets were allowed to operate as if they were private businesses. Thus taxi service was monopolized by the larger fleet operations which were able to make private contracts with hotels, restaurants, railroads and theaters for the use of their services. The following companies were the major fleet operators prior to World War I:

Yellow Taxicab Co.

Universal Taximeter Cab Co.

Motor Taximeter Cab Co.

Garden Taxicab Co.

Mason Seaman Transportation Co.

Haverty's Taxicabs Incorporated

New Taxicab and Auto Company

Forty-Seventh Street Taxicab Co.

Riverside Taxi Service Co.[6]

These companies operated from private hack stands located primarily in front of expensive hotels and offered the guests of the hotel the assurance that their drivers were honest and trustworthy. Fleet operators paid dearly for this privilege as the City Ordinance of 1913 recounts:

"Under the present private hack stand system all of the most lucrative hack stand business is practically monopolized by those companies and business

organizations which control the private stands, which companies pay the owners of the property abutting on the street where the private hack stand is located usually 10 per cent of their gross income from the stand, which amounts to a sum variously estimated from $350,000 upwards yearly."[7]

The private hack stand system could not and did not last in the face of the rising demand for taxi service. The private stand was abolished in August of 1913 due to the feeling that this system was responsible for the high rates and low number of taxis servicing the city.[8] Furthermore, drivers who did not work for companies leasing desirable hack stand space were at an extreme disadvantage, since the city had inadvertently allowed public property to be used for private gain by failing to realize the public nature of streets, avenues, thoroughfares, etc.

The elimination of private monopolies on public streets in 1913 concomitantly redefined the nature of public and private transportation service. It was felt that those who solicited business upon the public streets were engaged in a public employment and therefore should be licensed and regulated by the city in the best interests of the public, while private liveries obtaining business by prearrangement or on private property were outside of the scope of public regulation.[9] This established the taxi industry as a public concern and relegated the private liveries to a minor role in providing vehicular service. Those companies providing service exclusively to private hack stands were forced to become public carriers or to develop businesses outside of the realm of public interest.

The private hack stand created an artificial monopoly over the "production" of taxi service. The elimination of the fleet monopolies as a result, increased the number of owner driven taxis within the industry. No longer could a large fleet corner the market on public thoroughfares or streets. Nevertheless, certain forms of private hack stands continued to exist after countermanding legislation. These were allowed to exist on private property, such as railroad and steamship landings, as long as they did not solicit patronage upon the streets and did not have a taximeter attached.

The private livery's right to operate on private property, but with a public interest, was short lived. In the fall of 1917 the city redefined a Public Hack as:

> Any vehicle plying for hire, for which public patronage is solicited upon the street; any vehicle carrying passengers for hire operating from or in a railroad station or steamship landing.[10]

All vehicles possessing taximeters soliciting patronage upon the street or at railroad or steamship landings came within the jurisdiction of the Bureau of Licenses of the Mayor's office.

Broadway and 39th Street. The horse and wagon, trolley, two electric cabs (one a hansom and the other a brougham) were all means of transportation in 1887 before the advent of the gas-powered taxicab. (Photograph by Byron, The Byron Collection, Museum of the City of New York)

The livery's domain was sizably reduced by this law. Legally, he was only able to operate from a central garage contracting for its services in advance. Soon thereafter, the livery vehicle lost its prominence within the busy downtown section of the city and operated in the outer boroughs where taxi service was minimal. Having been preempted of the right to serve the lucrative Manhattan hotels, restaurants, theaters, railroads and steamship landings, the private livery enterprise was forced to operate on the fringes of the city in areas uncontested by the taxicab.

The breakup of fleet monopolies had severe economic repercussions within the industry. Several fleets folded, subsequent to the passage of the 1913 ordinance, since they no longer had an assured income connected with private stands, and also because the taxi drivers were demanding higher wages at a time when the city ordinance had reduced the fare rate structure of the industry.[11]

The city administration had felt that the private hack stand concessions had unnecessarily raised the cost of service to the public. Furthermore, there were charges of graft involved in the functioning of the privately operated stands which compounded the cost inefficiency of their operations. In the case of Yellow Taxicab Co. vs. Gaynor, the situation was summarized:

> When it is realized that the rates heretofore prevailing were necessarily so high as not only to pay a fair profit to those rendering service but also to defray the large sums which these persons were accustomed to pay to those operating hotels in front of whose premises private hack stands were established, it is easy to understand that the rates heretofore prevailing represented a profit upon something other than the cost of rendering the service.[12]

Mayor Gaynor felt that reduced rates could be furnished in New York City more easily than elsewhere "because of the density of traffic."[13] This, indeed, is what makes the New York taxi industry unique in America. Although the cost of operating a fleet may be higher in New York, the cost efficiency measured in terms of paid miles to total miles driven is much better.

As a result, the city reduced the cost of a taxi ride in 1913 and decreed that all taxi companies would charge 50 cents a mile for two passenger taxis and 70 cents a mile for three passenger taxis.[14] This was a sizable reduction in the cost of riding by cab, amounting to as much as a 50 percent saving over the previous rates. This daring move on the part of the city administration revolutionized the role of the old hansom cabs; rather than catering to the whims and tastes of the wealthy, they became an integral part of the mass transportation of New York. With these reduced rates, the demand for taxi service grew steadily after World War I. Nearly everybody was riding by cabs and often depending upon their services to supplement those of the subways.

From a private luxury oriented service, the taxi had been transformed overnight into a public form of travel. They had become a pervasive if not an annoying part of the city's landscape by 1920 when as many as 15,000 taxicabs were licensed to ply the streets;[15] a dramatic increase from the original 50 Darracq taxis operated by Mr. Allen in 1907.

Role Of Automobile Manufacturers: Competition, Rate Wars and Crime

During the twenties, automobile manufacturers began to realize the importance of developing outlets for their products. An increasing number of taxi fleets during the post World War I era came under the control of major automobile manufacturers. Checker Cab Company, General Motors, Dodge Motors, Ford Motor Co. and others saw the value of controlling large taxi fleets as a means for creating an established demand for their goods. As a consequence, many automobile manufacturers created subsidiary corporations controlled by the manufacturing concern for the sole purpose of dumping automobiles onto the streets of New York. Because this practice had been in effect for many years it became a significant determinant of the character and structure of taxi service in the twenties. In addition to supplying the vehicles for their own subsidiaries, these manufacturing concerns provided taxis for independent operators and other competing fleet owners, which led many of the large manufacturers into direct control over large segments of the industry. The easy payment terms they allowed induced many taxi owners to increase the size of their fleet, which in turn gave the manufacturers a greater market. Those owners unable to meet payments were completely at the mercy of the automobile manufacturers since their taxis could be recalled at any moment, or they could be forced to operate their vehicles at rates dictated through the subsidiary taxi company owned by the manufacturer. If competition became stiff, they could eliminate their competitors. Under these conditions repossession became a means for expanding their subsidiary company's holdings and dictating economic policies to the industry. The manufacturer could easily force his competitors to oppose unionization, limit wages or fall in line with whatever policy suited their interests. The manufacturer monopoly loomed as the greatest threat to free enterprise in the taxi industry.

However, the dramatic and excessive increase in the number of taxicabs in New York during the twenties was not totally helpful to the manufacturing concerns. By glutting the market with an excessive supply of cabs, they were jeopardizing the value of their investments. Too much competition was detrimental to the entire industry. There was not much that could be done since there were no restrictions on becoming a cab owner or driver prior to 1937. Anybody and everbody who wanted to drive a cab could do so.

Inevitably the larger fleets turned to rate wars as a solution.[16] As early as the summer of 1924 several of the large companies reduced their rates, by as much as 50 percent for the first mile of travel. Rather than paying 50 cents a mile, it became 25 cents a mile.

At this point all hell broke loose in the taxi industry. Rate reductions coupled with false advertising, gouging, cheating and extortion within the ranks of the hack profession gave the industry an image from which it has never fully recovered. Soon after the 25 cent rates were put into effect, they were further reduced to 10 cents a half mile, making them the lowest in the country.[17] This had the positive effect of stimulating taxi riding, but it also severely destroyed service. A cab rider could no longer be certain whether the cab he was hailing was going to charge a reduced rate, the normal rate for a two passenger cab, the normal rate for a three passenger cab, or whether the driver would take the opportunity to "gouge" his fare in light of all the confusion.

Some of the larger fleets who balked at reducing their rates suffered badly. Yellow Taxicab Corporation, in particular, was severely annoyed at the whole situation, feeling the rate cutting campaign was suicidal. The real culprits were the taxicab manufacturers who had promoted the rate slashing as a means of disposing of an enormous overstock of their automobiles. With little concern for the economics of the independent or small fleet owner, the city had allowed the large manufacturers to ramrod their rates into existence, creating a full scale rate war within the industry.

The taxicab war beginning in the summer of 1924 left a trail of crime and corruption for nearly a full year, although the effect was to democratize taxi transportation. As the *New York Times* of August 1924 states:

> People who never did anything more than dodge taxicabs are riding in them, those who hailed them on gala occasions are using them as a regular thing.[18]

With the price of a taxi ride as cheap as the 5 cent subway ride, an enormous number of people began riding by taxi. An estimated 300,000 people used taxis daily in 1924—a 30 percent increase in the demand for cabs over the prior normal rates.[19]

Nevertheless, the city administration soon realized that the chaotic situation caused by the rate wars was doing more damage than mere confusion. The rate wars instituted by the manufacturers did promote the use of their cabs, but it also destroyed any semblence of honesty and decency among the hack profession. Their natural inclinations to cheat, hustle and steal were given a strong boost by the "subway rates" then in effect. Furthermore, the confusion of the rate wars had created as many as six different costs for the price of a taxi ride and an equal number of ways of being swindled.

It was at this time that the police department stepped into the industry to eliminate the gangsters, crooks, and racketeers disguised as public hacks. To the police department, taxis and crime were almost synonymous terms. They had watched the industry grow from an infant to a giant by the mid twenties, accompanied by a similar growth in its rackets and crime.[20] In effect, the taxi industry had been developed into a massive public transportation system without developing any public regulations over the fleet owner or his drivers.

At the insistence of Chief City Magistrate William McAdoo, the Taxi Industry was placed under police jurisdiction in the spring of 1925. McAdoo had long felt that the public prominence of hacks had caused them to commit more crimes and aid in the process of crime more than those of any other occupation. McAdoo rightly sensed that the independence of the hack profession facilitated careers for criminals. As he stated:

> The taxicab in the hands of a man of dangerous character and criminal tendencies is one of the most efficient aids to the commission of crime that is known to the police.[21]

The New York Taxi industry, though the greatest in the country, if not in the world, was overrun by gangsters. These men were either in league with hacks or hacks themselves and went far beyond the normal and assumed rate gouging that victimized the passenger. More important was the fact that gangsters were using the taxi as part of their burglaries and bank jobs to make quick getaways. As Police Commissioner Enright stated in 1925:

> In thousands of cases during the last seven years we have found that criminals were using taxicabs in connection with burglaries, holdups, safe-blowing jobs and other criminal enterprises of the first magnitude.

The growth of the use of the taxi had increased their criminal use. The mass production of service had inadvertently become a mass production of crime.

It appears likely that the large automotive manufacturers permitted this criminal ambience to develop within the industry through the manner in which they conducted business. The large manufacturers not only flooded the industry with cabs, but also owned and controlled the large taxi fleets. The manufacturers gave little thought to the latent consequences of reducing rates. One such effect was to increase cheating by drivers. Nor did they give any serious attention to the qualifications of the taxi drivers.[22] Only when the son of a prominent New Yorker was killed by a cab driver, did anyone notice the industry had become run by hoodlums. This was a major event and it sparked the otherwise leathargic municipal assembly to pass legislation placing the police department in charge of the hack profession. In fact, Mayor Hylan justified the legislation in light of the murder of Dennis Kenny who had been shot in February of 1925 by an unlicensed taxicab chauffeur.

During the following years the police eliminated several thousand unlicensed drivers who had been allowed to work by fleet owners intent upon keeping their cabs on the street at whatever cost. Under police rule, cab fares were standardized and the price of a taxi ride was placed at 40 cents a mile.[23]

During the years 1925 to 1930 the number of taxicabs rose from 20,000 to over 30,000 at its peak.[24] In less than ten short years the automobile manufacturers had added as many as 15,000 more taxicabs to the streets of New York. They were relentlessly turning out more amd more automobiles and nobody quite knew what to do with all of them. They were crowding the streets and creating a general nuisance, the likes of which New York has not since seen. Even the automotive manufacturers soon realized that they had overdone it; their investments were not turning into profit and rate wars did not offer a solution.

Regulation and Corruption:
Mayor Walker Sets Future Pattern

In 1930 Mayor Walker set about to determine proper regulations to govern the industry. His Taxicab Commission came up with the conclusion that the Taxi Industry ought to be run by large scale fleets under a semimonopolistic system. They recommended that the Taxicab Industry be declared a public utility and be regulated under a Taxicab Control Board. In fact, the commission concluded that a unification of the city's taxicab service under a single franchised corporation would be the best system.[25] By this position the Walker Taxicab Commission was directly advocating the elimination of owner-drivers from the industry and a takeover by the large fleet companies who operated as subsidiaries of the automobile manufacturing concerns. It sounded like a perfect dream of monopoly which the major manufacturers had long been seeking. It was somewhat surprising that the Walker Commission, supposedly a non-partisan public group, should have been the proponent of the manufacturers' rather than the public's viewpoint.

Mayor Walker signed the Taxicab control law in January of 1932 after months of heated debate surrounding its passage.[26] Those in favor of it, of course, were the large fleets, while those against it were the independent operators. However, in the month of May of 1932 the whole plot was laid bare.

Mayor Walker had been bribed to create the Taxicab Control Commission to establish a monopoly situation for the large fleet corporations.[27] It was a national scandal, since in a presidential election year it brought Governor Roosevelt into the embarrassing position of presiding over the "sickening corruption" which characterized the government of New York City. The initial inquiry into the taxicab bribery led to a far-reaching indictment of the Walker Administration and his eventual resignation from office in September of 1932.

Samuel Seabury, the chief counsel for the investigation of the Taxicab scandal, indicted the Walker regime for its close association with the underworld and organized crime. In fact, Seabury was adamant in showing that organized government had become a branch of organized crime. As he stated to the American Law Institute:

> Organized government today is confronted with the task of dealing with organized crime. Especially is this so in some of our great cities, where the forces of the underworld are effectively organized and often act in cooperation with the local political machines which masquerade under the name of a political party. . . . These underworld forces are in many respects better organized than are the forces of law and order. They have no rules that impede their efforts in achieving their purposes.

The major piece of evidence against Mayor Walker was the gift of $26,-535 worth of bonds he received from a taxi financier named J. A. Sisto. Mr. Sisto, a partner in the firm J. A. Sisto & Co. had been responsible for issuing the securities of the Checker Cab Manufacturing Company, the owner of the Parmalee subsidiary, which in turn operated the New York subsidiary, Yellow Taxi Corporation. Sisto's $26,535 bribe was made to insure the passage by the mayor of the Taxicab Control bill, designed to turn the industry into a massive privately owned monopoly.[29]

Sisto, it was learned, had been in close touch with Morris Markin, president of the Checker Cab Manufacturing Company and had been advised by Mr. Markin that regulatory controls were a good thing for the taxicab industry. In particular Mr. Markin emphasized that regulatory controls might not be for the good of the taxi industry as a whole but that they were quite good for large taxi companies. The passage of the Taxicab Control bill inevitably meant an increase in the value of the Checker manufactured cabs in the city of New York. The municipally created legislation directly benefited the Checker Cab Manufacturing Corporation and further increased the value of the Checker securities, floated on the market by the J. A. Sisto Company.

A further indictment of the Taxicab Control law came with the confession made by B. M. Seymour, vice president of the Terminal Cab Company. He acknowledged to Mr. Seabury that a Senator Hastings was being paid $18,000 a year simply to promote taxi legislation favorable to his company. In fact, Seymour admitted that Mr. Hastings was being paid more money than he himself received as the vice president of the company. Mr. Seabury found that the Terminal Cab Company had previously attempted to make political inroads into Tammany Hall but because the Parmalee Transportation and Yellow Cab Company had been firmly in control of the political scene there for a number of years, only a few options short of outright bribery were available. As Mr. Seymour confessed during the trial:

> Yes, I was quite certain that he could be of assistance. I knew Senator Hastings was a politician. It was obvious by the office which he holds, and that our competitor—at least we had reason to believe—was well entrenched politically. They had been in business here for a great many years, and it was a factor that we could not be unmindful of.[30]

The $18,000 "investment" of Mr. Seymour was a clever means for gaining greater control of the city's taxi business through political legislation and, more significantly, achieving a taxi monopoly from which to reap greater profits.

Despite these blatant corporate measures to control taxi legislation in New York City, the Taxicab Board of Control was hailed by many as a positive first step within the industry. Even owner drivers, after several months of appraisal, began to see that Maurice Hotchner, Chairman of the Board was not submitting to the demands of the large fleet interests. However, many drivers rightly sensed that the Taxicab Board of Control had to hold a strong anti-monopoly position in light of the public indictment of the Walker regime and the Taxicab Board itself. Although the Board took a firm anti-monopoly stand, it was abolished along with two other Walker created city bureaus in December of 1932 to alleviate the large debt burdening the city during the depression.[31] These drastic city reforms were more than mere economy measures; they were a statement by the succeeding regime that organized crime and coercion were to be eliminated from the city politic. The Taxicab Board of Control, despite its attempts to prove its public worth, was deeply rooted in scandal. Its mere existence implied corruption. Nobody was willing to idolize the Board after it had been dragged through all the courts and had been ritually spit upon by all its opponents.

After the Walker scandal, anti-monopoly became the catch all phrase in all legislative attempts to improve the business image of the taxi industry. The city council carefully avoided favoring legislation which permitted monopoly to develop within the industry. Their fear of the consequences of private monopoly, which had nearly taken over the industry during the Walker regime, made them wary of passing any more legislation. However, within five years of the abolition of the Taxicab Board of Control, monopoly reared its head once again.

Restriction of Competition: The Medalion

The second major legal transformation of the taxi industry occured on March 9, 1937. The City Council passed a bill supported by Alderman Lew Haas to limit the number of taxicabs in the city of New York to the number presently in operation. The intent of the legislation was to reduce the competition on the streets, raise the drivers' income, reduce traffic congestion and eliminate the copying of color schemes and emblems previously assigned to certain taxicab owners.[32]

At the time, however, the underlying fear of most of the Aldermen was the emergence of a taxicab monopoly. By freezing the number of owner-driven taxis and fleet taxis, it was felt that no monopolies could develop. Nevertheless, there was the nagging fear that the Haas Act alone could not prevent this possibliity. For this reason the legislative findings included the following:

> The present ratio existing between the two types of owners is fair and equitable and should be preserved. It is further found that in limiting the number of taxicabs, the public and the taxicab industry must be safeguarded against the ultimate possibliity of monopolistic control, with its attendent evils.[33]

The basis on which the city council passed the bill was relatively unscientific and unenlightened. Their fear of monopoly had been so strong they inadvertently created the devil they wished to destroy. They legislated against the possiblity of a private monopoly controlled by the large fleets by creating a government cartel which sanctioned the monopoly of the entire taxi industry. The fears of the depression and post depression era provoked many legislative attempts to protect businesses fraught with a public interest. In essence, the limitations the taxi industry now lives with were products of the highly unstable and bleak economic picture of the thirties. The fear of control by a few was, in reality, a paranoia of the times. In fact, there were more owner-driven taxis during the 1930s than in any other period of the New York taxi industry. The report of the Mayor's Commission on Taxicabs stated in 1930 that 52 percent of all the taxis were fleet owned and that:

> Only 26 percent of the cabs are in fleets of 100 or more and these are divided among 11 different operations.[34]

A mere four years later 54 percent of all the taxis were fleet owned and again only 26 percent of all the taxis were owned in fleets of 100 or more although this time these were divided between two different operations: The Parmalee system, a subsidiary of the Checker Corporation, and the Terminal Transportation Systems, Inc., a subsidiary of the General Motors Corporation.[35]

Although two fleets had gained control over the large scale operations in the city, the actual proportion of fleet cabs to owner-driven cabs and the relative strength of the large fleet operators to the small fleet operators remained unchanged.

The Haas Act, however, stabilized the relative strength of the fleet owner. With its passage, the fleets increased their size relative to the owner drivers, controlling 61 percent of the industry. They also coalesced into one organization: The Metropolitan Taxi Board of Trade. It became the single bargaining agent for the entire city's fleet operations, negotiating for fare rates and determining the proper wages to be paid to the drivers.

Paradoxically, a monopoly had emerged without anyone in the city administration taking notice. From 1937 to the present, the New York public has directly paid for the administrative blunder of the Haas Act with higher fares and poorer service. It is ironic that in 1934 the Mayor's Commission on Taxicabs envisioned the unsalutary effects of the Haas Act. As the report so vividly stated:

> The inevitable result of limiting the number of medallions to be issued at any one time would mean that every present owner of a medallion would hang on to it like grim death in the hope that someone else would be forced to surrender his medallions first, and the person who could hang on the longest would reap the benefit of reduction.[36]

The rise in the value of the medallion for both fleets and owner-drivers inevitably accompanied the passage of the Haas Act in the post World War II era. The industry was quite content since there had been an enormous upswing in the demand for taxi service.

In turn, the strong demand for taxi service quickly made the medallion a more valuable commodity. From the original $10 price paid for the medallion in 1937, the price had soared to as high as $10,000 by 1950.[37] Overnight it had become a sacred and much prized commodity. Fleet owners were well aware of its value, which in turn made them fearful of putting their assets (represented by the medallion) on the public streets without adequate protection. The fleet owners soon found the solution in the year 1952.

The Fleet Holding Company: Device to Limit Passenger Liability

Fleet taxis are insured up to $10,000 against all personal injuries and accidents. In addition, many larger and more lucrative cab companies file bonds guaranteeing payment of that amount for injury to one person. Nevertheless, fleet insurance policies involve slightly more than mere protection of the public. By filing a bond, the fleet owner is able to avoid paying the premium for insurance which would otherwise be required by law. Subsequent to the 1952 fare hike fleet taxis operated with a separate corporation for every two to three taxis within the fleet.[38] By this device of a holding company, the vulnerability of the principal owner(s) of the entire fleet has been minimized, since his assets are held by separate corporations that in turn limit the liability of the overall fleet. Thus a fleet of 150 cabs will generally have as many as 75 corporations representing its fleet. This procedure protects the fleet against loss of their total liabilities due to suits by the taxi-riding public as a result of substantial personal injury. It is a form of legal hocus pocus which allows the fleet owners to conveniently side-step responsibility for the carelessness of their drivers. The fleet is extremely vulnerable at this very point, since accidents are a frequent occurrence among taxi drivers.[39] Furthermore, many fleet drivers are inexperienced cab drivers due to their limited number of days of driving and their limited stay within the industry.[40] As a result, the owner adjusts to the erratic driving habits and high accident proneness of the drivers by limiting his legal liability to the injured party. Instead of taking responsibility for his drivers, he passes the responsibility over to the unsuspecting public. In 1958 in the case of Teller vs. Clear Service Co., the court found that there had been increasing concealment of fleet assets through corporate veils over the years. In 1937 8,424 taxicabs were owned by 380 corporate fleet owners. In 1958, although the total number of fleet owned taxicabs was reduced to 6,816, the actual number of corporations owning this smaller number of cabs was increased from 380 to 2,120. At that time only 332 of the 2,120 corporations owned more than one taxicab. The decision in the case stated:

> Although the increase in the number of corporations and the reduction of the number of taxicabs registered in the name of each may, in some instances, have been partially motivated by the legitimate desire to reduce federal income taxes (the corporate federal income tax provided for a tax of 30 per cent on income up to $25,000 per year, whereas the tax is 52 per cent on income over that amount), it is clear that the predominant motive, generally has been the desire to avoid recovery of more than nominal or negligible amounts on judgements obtained for negligent operation of the taxicabs.[41]

The desire to protect the value of the medallion investment through multicorporate veils became a fashion right about the time of the fare rate hike of 1952, the first increase in the value of the medallion investment since 1937. As a result, the 25 percent increase in the cost of a taxi ride heightened the value of the medallion and made the fleet owners more sensitive to possible accident and personal injury suits which could wipe out their entire fleet. The more valuable their medallions became, the more corporate armor they shoved between themselves and the taxi-riding public. It is naive to believe that the passenger riding in a New York cab is adequately protected against the recklessness of the driver. One can be sure that if the driver is not going to be careful with his passenger, the fleet owner is much less willing to protect him. The corporate fraud of fleet owners is not a minor backroom affair. It affects millions of New Yorkers every day, since the taxicab industry is a public transportation service upon which the city has grown to rely. In the case of Teller vs. Clear Service Co., the judge said:

> That the public is inadequately protected with respect to compensation for personal injuries sustained through the negligence of taxicab . . . and the state and the city are unwitting accomplices of a legalized racket to avoid liability for payment for the negligent maiming and killing by taxicabs.[42]

Furthermore, in 1965 in the case of Mull vs. Colt Co. Inc., they decided that:

> The industry generally has demonstrated an appalling lack of concern for the public and has been guilty of so shameful an exercise in immorality that it almost defies description.[43]

Through the use of corporate armor, the liability of the fleet owners for accidents is limited as well as the risk of bankruptcy. The owner is thereby assured that no matter how bad his drivers are and regardless of the extent of the accident, he will never lose more than two taxicabs and the $10,000 bond filed to guarantee payment for damages.[44] Incorporation thus enables the owner to avoid placing the true value of all his medallioned assets in the hands of every careless driver employed by his fleet. The drivers may cheat on the owner, but the taxi riding public will rarely get the same opportunity in the event of a serious accident. Although taxis are an integral part of the New York City transportation system, the required insurance coverage on taxis is equivalent to the minimum required on a private automobile. Surely this is tantamount to publicly legitimated fraud and irresponsibility.

Public interest within the taxi industry has been controlled through the political corruption of the fleet owner, his corporate structure and the political and economic power of the largest automobile manufacturers operating in New York. However, the exploitation of the public for private gain has not been limited to the passenger; it has also victimized the owner's partner—the driver.

4

Genealogy Of Unionization

From Underworld Locals
To National Racketeering

Besides protecting the value of the fleet medallion from public liability incurred through accidents, the owners have been equally concerned with protecting the value of their monopoly from the grips of an effective labor contract. The owner's willingness to sabotage the basic tenets of collective bargaining is indicative of his desire to control the economic structure of the industry.

In the early days of the industry, the political power of the large taxicab manufacturers placed the fate of labor in the hands of a small group of men. By 1930, 75 percent of all the taxicabs in New York were produced by taxicab manufacturers and 26 percent of all the fleet taxis were directly owned by manufacturing interests. This gave a small group of men direct or indirect control over the vast majority of fleet operated taxis. The manufacturer simply dictated labor policy to the industry knowing full well that no one could afford to contravene his decision. Those who opposed the manufacturer were faced with the possibility of losing their taxicabs for failure to meet their payments. This power laid most of the early unions to rest.

Prior to the Haas Act of 1937 all efforts to organize the cab driver were rather disorganized and provincial. Most early unions approached the task by organizing individual companies rather than trying to organize the entire city's taxi labor force. This provincial orientation to the taxicab profession divided the city's cabbies from each other and hindered the development of any sense of brotherhood among drivers.

Effect of the Commission System on Unionization

The first attempt to organize the fleet drivers came several years after the introduction of the automotive taxi into New York. At this time the Chauffeurs and Helpers Union was attempting to gain control of the industry at a time when the industry itself was collapsing from the strain of overcompetition.[1] Prior to 1913 owners had been dependent upon the use of private hack stands for virtually all of their business. When the city council eliminated the private hack stand concession and made them a public concern, drivers previously working for a fleet operation were lured into starting their own businesses. The union was weakened by this development, since the advantages of becoming an independent driver outweighed the benefits a union could bestow on its membership. In effect, the union was left without a strong bargaining position once the fleet-owned taxis were deprived of their control over lucrative hack stands.

Nevertheless, two years later in 1915 the leaders of the Chauffeurs Division of the International Brotherhood of Teamsters had managed to organize five major fleets in the city and were in the process of demanding an increase in salary from the only non-unionized fleet, The Mason Seaman Transportation Company. Unfortunately the union's demands for a higher salary of $3 for a ten-hour day proved to be economically too difficult to handle with the 50 percent reduction in taxicab rates that went into effect in the summer of 1913. Moreover, union demands and excessive work stoppages caused by strikes within the industry had inadvertently forced several of the major fleets to close shop.

Under the Chauffeurs and Helpers Union, the taxi drivers operated on a fixed salary system from 1911 to 1921.[2] A driver was paid a daily salary and in turn was required to work a fixed number of hours per day. the original contract called for a $2.53 wage for an 11-hour day. A second contract was ratified in the fall of 1916 increasing the drivers' income from

23 cents an hour for an 11-hour day ($2.53) to 25 cents an hour for a ten hour day ($2.50).[3]

Fleet owners were not at all happy with the fixed salary system then in operation. They proposed a commision system as early as the spring of 1917 which they felt would reduce their fixed costs and give the drivers an incentive to make more money.[4] Interestingly enough their proposal was turned down by the union, since it felt the traffic congestion and the geography of the city would work against drivers.

As early as 1919 the Teamsters Local 267 began fading in importance and company unions or associations began taking over the industry. The first company union was the Black and White Chauffeurs Association which negotiated exclusively with the Black and White Taxicab Company.[5]

The Black and White Chauffeurs successfully managed an increase in their income prior to the spring of 1921. The company made the first step toward a commission system by guaranteeing a minimum $4.50 per day and 20 percent commission on all monies above $80 per week. This system, however, promoted a great deal of reckless driving, since it required each driver to bring in a minimum of $80 per week or lose his job. Under this contract, the fleet owner was virtually assured of making a profit since every driver's job was at stake if he did not produce the desired bookings for the company. This system soon met its demise, for the following year all of the major fleets began offering strictly a commission system of wages with a minimum production quota attached. A driver was no longer assured of a minimum wage under the commission system which, in effect, worked to the owners' advantage since it eliminated the "bad bookers" and prompted drivers to work as hard for the boss as they did for themselves. Under this contract, the owner had no fixed overhead and was assured a minimum production of money from each of his drivers, or they would be fired. The commission rate in the fall of 1922 varied from 33.3 percent to 40 percent depending upon the fleet and the required mimimum production quota per week.[6] For the most part drivers were receiving either 33.3 percent or 35 percent of the total amount of money earned on the street.

In the fall of 1923 another company union was created to deal with the Mogul Checker Cab Corporation. The Brotherhood of Taxi Chauffeurs of Greater New York as it was called, was not very effective, although it did manage to gain a modicum of support in four major fleets then existing in New York. This company union managed to raise the commission from 35 percent in 1923 to 40 percent in 1924 with a clause that night drivers would still receive only 35 percent of the commission. Moreover, this contract also provided for a 50-50 split for all monies above and beyond $90 per week.[7]

During the next nine years from 1925 to 1934 many individual attempts were made to create a union within specific fleets, but these efforts all failed. The Hackmen's Protective Association, the International Brotherhood of Teamsters,[8] as well as the Union of Taxicab and Bus Drivers of Greater New York all attempted to gain recognition within the industry between 1925 and 1929, but were driven out of the business due to the lack of driver support.[9] Like all previous company unions that sprang up during the twenties, these organizations dealt with local shop conditions rather than with the pervasive and common labor problems of the industry.

Company unions which were concerned with the workplace as the focus of organizing attempts soon lost power and popularity with the onset of the depression in the early thirties. In the following years the hack profession as opposed to the particular workplace of individual taxi drivers became the focus for major citywide organizing attempts. These citywide attempts at unionization were, to say the least, a major break with the traditional means of organizing cab drivers. On the surface it might appear that these citywide efforts, which began in 1934, revealed a developing class consciousness among cab drivers as to their common lot. Although there were strong communist forces within the American labor movement and the taxi industry at this time the majority of drivers were less inclined to believe in class solidarity than in the value of a better contract. It was only coincidentally that many cab drivers allied themselves with communist organizers during this period when wages were at a shockingly low level.

The tendency to citywide unionization undoubtedly was reinforced by the creation of the National Recovery Administration in 1933 which supported labor's right to strike. Furthermore, the depression years were ripe for labor organizing within the industry since wages were low and there were an abundant number of radical labor organizers within the industry.

Perhaps the most violent and dramatic attempt to unionize the industry during the depression came in the spring of 1934 when drivers protested a five cents tax to be placed on the price of a taxi ride. As many as 12,000 cabs went on strike on February 2, 1934 to thwart the proposed tax, since the fleet owners proposed to split the tax 60-40 with the driver.[10] The drivers had no intentions at all of sharing the nickel with the boss especially after Mayor La Guardia had taken their side and insisted on returning the entire proceeds of the tax to them. As a result of this confusion, four separate organizations were formed: The United Taxi Drivers Union in Brooklyn, The Empire Taxi Chauffeurs Union in the Bronx, The Taxi Workers Union, and the Chauffeurs Protective Association, all of which coalesced into the Central Taxicab Committee of 13 representing a total of 20,000 drivers throughout the city.[11] Mayor La Guardia initially supported the unionizing efforts and felt that the drivers ought to get AFL support. Despite its size, the Central Taxicab Committee was unable to obtain recognition from the fleet owners of New York. Instead the fleet owners countered with the threat, "either you return to work or you're fired."

The nickel tax issue was resolved on February 8 with the drivers receiving 50 percent of the fund collected. Nevertheless, the fleet owners were still unwilling to recognize the union. As happened countless times in the past, the fleet owners used the standard subterfuge, claiming that they would recognize the union if it were actually representative.[12] Obviously, arguments of this kind left the fleet driver powerless to negotiate.

Although the taxi strike ended on February 8,[13] the issue of union recognition continued to plague the industry for another two months, in which time the industry witnessed some of the worst violence and hostility ever seen in the taxi industry's history. Further grounds for conflict arose in the following month when the United Taxi Drivers Union of Greater New York contended that Parmalee Systems drivers were not truly being represented by the shop union, known as the Drivers Brotherhood of Parmalee Systems. They insisted that the shop union was in collusion with the management and therefore ought to be eliminated and replaced by their union. Fleet owners were unwilling to recognize or negotiate with the new union. This, in turn, prompted three weeks of indiscriminate violence on the part of the fleet drivers, further damaging their union's image in the eyes of the fleet owner.[14]

The Underworld Takes Its Commission

During this period, much was said and done within the ranks of fleet drivers to permanently damage the hope of unionization in the near or distant future of the taxi industry. Both fleet owners and drivers were accused of being run by sinister forces, according to Aldermanic President Bernard Deutsch. Chicago racketeers, Communist infiltrators, and gangsters were blamed for the worst disruption to take place in the history of the taxi industry.[15] Communist infiltrators were blamed for much of the internal dissension prevailing among hackmen, although District Attorney Foley credited gangsters with directing some of the strike disorders in the Bronx under the tutelage of Ciro Terranova, the "Artichoke King," so-called because of his control of the city's artichoke peddlers.

Much of the problem behind the attempted unionization of fleet drivers was due to the presence of underworld labor racketeers within the industry. In fact, one of the key union leaders during the strikes of 1934, Samuel Smith, president of the Independent Taxicab Union, was indicted in 1938 by District Attorney Thomas E. Dewey as part of a one million dollar taxicab racket.[16] Dewey claimed that underworld leaders formerly affiliated with Lucky Luciano were solely responsible for the violence and sabotage that characterized the New York taxicab strikes in 1934. He further explained that these underworld leaders were using the union label as a front to extort monies in dues from the drivers and were operating a loan sharking business on the side.

The loan sharking operation began in 1935 and became so merciless by 1936 that it was brought to the attention of District Attorney Thomas E. Dewey who stated that those borrowing money were paying $6 weekly for

The taxi strike of 1934 came at the height of the depression when wages were at the "starvation minimum" and the Mafia was beginning to take over the union. (New York Daily News Photo)

every $5 borrowed with the usury progressing through the default of payments until the interest reached as much as 1,040 percent on loans.[17]

The underworld managed taxi union was connected to some of the most powerful industrial racketeers of the twenties and thirties. Sam Smith, president of the Independent Taxicab Union was affiliated with Jake (Gurrah) Shapiro, who happened to be his brother-in-law, and Lewis (Lepke) Buchalter, the most powerful racketeer in New York between 1927 and 1936.[18] Lepke and Gurrah were alleged to have extorted between five and ten million dollars annually from the small businesses of New York; although, some of their income was derived from their narcotics racket. Lepke was intimately connected with many of the other powerful underworld figures of the day, such as Lansky and Luciano. However, his personal power was closely connected to his industrial rackets within the Garment industry.

The underworld union managed by Sam Smith was part of this larger criminal syndicate managed by Jake Shapiro and Lepke. Lepke managed to avoid any immediate connections with the taxi industry during the time he developed his taxicab racket in the early thirties. Instead he dictated his ruthless policies of extortion and coercion through an organization of about 25 men who could call upon the services of a small army of guerillas at any time for "special assignments." These special assignments usually involved intimidating helpless owners into paying them dues on a regular basis, or as in the case of the taxicab industry, the Lepke gang went through the formality of creating a "protective association" which forced the unwilling owners to pay "dues" to ensure that nothing happened to their taxicabs, garages or drivers.

Another aspect of their taxicab racket involved dictating where fleet owners could buy their gasoline, insurance and supplies. This aspect of the Lepke operation was designed to throw most of the important business into the hands of Lepke controlled suppliers who began catering to the needs of the taxi industry in the early part of 1935.[19]

Having enlisted more than 2,000 taxi drivers into the union during the 1934 strike Smith was able to charter his local and use it against the fleet owners as part of Lepke's industrial racket. In 1935 the union became the bargaining tool for Lepke's operations. At this time four companies owning over 60 percent of all the taxis in New York were forced to pay weekly 30 cents on each cab to the racketeers with the promise that their drivers and taxicabs would be immune from attacks of stench bombs, the ripping of upholstery and even the burning of cabs by guerillas in the hire of racketeers.[20] In 1937 the extortion scheme was accelerated to 50 cents on each cab, since the racketeers sensed that the end was near and consequently wanted to make a final grab from the companies involved in the scheme.

The presence of the underworld in the taxi industry during most of the thirties eliminated the possibility of an effective and representative union entering the field. Lepke's gang destroyed the 1934 hopes of collective bargaining through its underworld union and single handedly dictated the future of the industry from 1933 to 1937. This was done through The Taxicab Chauffeurs Union, Local 19795, chartered after the violent strikes of 1934 which became the right arm of underworld extortion within the industry until 1937 when its charter was revoked.[21]

Although the depression of the thirties was responsible for what one driver called the "starving wages," some of the problem can be attributed to the driver's inability to oust the underworld and organize an effective union. The fleet owners were able to maintain low wages during the thirties because there was no way the drivers could collectively employ their power while men like Lepke and Sam Smith preyed upon the industry. The depression of the thirties hit the cab driver worse than many other occupations, since these men had no labor contract and there were no limitations on the number of people who wished to drive a cab. The oversupply of labor coupled with a precipitous drop in the demand for taxi service pushed the daily wages of the cab driver to as low as $1.20 in 1934.[22] The condition of the cab driver was so severe during Lepke's reign that many of them were on relief.

However, for the fleet owners this oversupply of labor, reaching as high as 80,000 in 1931, was the key to their success.[23] With that many eligible drivers no fleet owner was in the least bit concerned with attempts at unionization, since threats of strike could be undermined by hiring a new labor force.

The Emergence of the Transport Workers: Consolidation of Power

The next significant and genuine attempt toward unionization came in the summer of 1937, a little over two months after the passage of the Haas Act limiting the number of taxicabs licensed by the city. This in theory was an ideal time to renew the unionization efforts, since a limitation on the absolute number of cabs could be coordinated with a closed shop agreement limiting the work force and strengthening the membership. The new union, called the Greater New York Taxicab Chauffeurs and Service Men, took over the Parmalee System and attempted to organize on a citywide basis. This local was a subdivision of the United Automobile Workers of America but it managed to gather additional support from The Transport Workers

Union under the reins of Mike Quill.[24] At this time The International Brotherhood of Teamsters was also trying their hand at unionizing the industry. The Teamsters Local 819, known as the Greater New York Taxi Chauffeurs and Taxi Service Men, in effect, proceeded to step into the shoes of the old company union, the Drivers Brotherhood of the Parmalee System, and signed a closed shop agreement with the Parmalee System in the summer of 1937.[25]

The UAW having temporarily lost control over the Parmalee drivers to the Teamster Local, handed control of the taxi industry over to the Transportation Workers Union, under the supervision of Mike Quill.[26] Under his direction, the TWU expanded its efforts to encompass all of the major fleets of the city. He managed to obtain the first collective bargaining referendum to be held in the taxicab field in the United States and was able to gain exclusive control of the Terminal Transportation System work force.[27] Within a month the TWU had organized over 9,000 drivers and proceeded to establish contracts with two other fleets. Under the TWU drivers were guaranteed $28 per week plus 40 per cent commissions on all earnings over $45 per week and day drivers were given $15 per week plus 40 percent commissions on all earnings over $37.50 per week. Adding to the Transport Workers' success, the Teamster's contract with the Parmalee System was declared void by the State Labor Relations Board, since no official election had been held to determine the right to collective bargaining.[28] As a result, an official election was held and the Transport Workers won by an overwhelming majority. This, in the opinion of the Transport Workers Union confirmed the fact that the Teamsters had ramrodded their way to control of the Parmalee System, or at least made a deal with the management for control of the drivers.[29]

By the beginning of October 1937, just five short months later, the Transport Workers had established a closed shop agreement with all but one of the major fleets. Their success was somewhat tenuous, however, since there was a great deal of internal dissent among the ranks of hackmen concerning the value and status of the union. In fact, on two separate occasions non-union inspired strikes erupted, which officials of the union blamed upon the fleet owners who were seeking a violation of the contract.

In December of 1937 a second contract on an industry-wide basis was negotiated with the Transport Workers Union affecting 15,000 drivers.[30] This contract was a major step in the evolution of the union's strength, since it was no longer divided by separate company contracts and wage clauses; instead the union managed to obtain a sliding wage scale based entirely on a commission system without any minimum wage provision or minimum booking provision. In effect the new contract instituted a 40 percent commission rate for all bookings under $27 a week and a 50 percent commission rate on all monies above that amount. Nevertheless, a certain hierarchy of status was maintained within the contract since night drivers were required to make $36 rather than $27 to be eligible for a 50 percent commission rate.

The Transport Workers' contract represented the first consolidation of labor power within the industry. The TWU's success in negotiating two contracts placed the drivers in a position of power which they had never known. The owners had always been able to take advantage of the cab driver because of his minor interest in the status of the profession and because the underworld figures like Lepke were able to deter the emergence of honest labor leaders. It was understandable that the fleet owners became quite apprehensive over the growing power of the taxi union since, for the first time in 30 years, their power had reached a parity with their own.

This growing union was not just a threat to the fleet owner's profits; it became a threat to the value of their monopoly created by the Haas Act just nine months earlier. The fleet owners interpreted the union's desire to increase wages as a threat to the monopoly the city had fostered through muncipal legislation.

Defeat and Decline of TWU

Two weeks after the second contract, a new contract was negotiated with four major taxi fleets calling for an increase in commissions to 42½ per cent for approximately 10,000 employees working 5,200 taxicabs.[31] This provision was significant because it attempted to do what no taxi union had ever done: eliminate all extra and part-time drivers and limit the union membership to a maximum of 15,000 full-time workers. This represented a reduction of nearly 30,000 drivers from the total 42,000 licensed hackmen and was soon to endanger the fleet owner's strength and economic security. Thus it was not a surprise in the spring of 1938 when the fleet owners categorically abolished minimum wages and eliminated the 2½ per cent commission increase agreed to two months before.[32] The fleet owners' representative justified the action as follows: "They had been forced to their action in order to forestall the financial ruin imminent to 50 companies bound by the recent agreement."[33]

Naturally, the broken contract precipitated strikes and hostility toward the ruthless policies of the fleet owner, yet within a short period the fleet owners had overruled the drivers' reaction and the industry was living under an unratified contract. The fleet owners' efforts to sabotage the union continued unchecked throughout all of 1938. Drivers were intimidated not to pay their dues, shop stewards were brutalized by fleet hired thugs, and many were forced to sign petitions denouncing the union if they wished to take out a cab.

The result of the fleet owners' efforts as well as the Union's precarious hold over its membership was the dissolution of the citywide control enjoyed by Transport Workers over the taxi industry. As early as January of 1939 new elections were held under the auspices of the New York State Labor Relations Board at the instigation of the fleet owners and several company unions. The election was tragic for the Transport Workers Union since it was only able to maintain sole bargaining authority over six out of the 28 fleets involved in the dispute. Company unions, like Metropolitan Taxi Workers Union which gained control of five fleets, and the Independent Taxicab Union were born from the remains of the Transport Workers Union's former membership and strength.[34] Although the TWU was soundly defeated by counter efforts of company unions or anti-unionists in a majority of garages, their victories took place in the larger fleets, which employed a greater number of drivers, and this consequently increased the value of these minor victories. In effect, they received 44 percent of all the votes.[35]

The Transport Workers had been progressively divided and conquered by the use of individual company elections rather than citywide elections for determining proper union representation. This technique of testing the Transport Workers' strength through continued fleet owner demands for elections brought TWU's power to an ebb during the war years. During World War II efforts at unionization subsided with the decrease in the number of cabs and drivers. The idea, however, was renewed soon afterwards in the fall of 1946 by a different union. John L. Lewis's District 50 division of the United Mine Workers stepped into the industry to begin organizing.[36]

The New York Industrial Union Local 13194, affiliated with the Mineworkers was specifically concerned with ousting the numerous company unions and grabbing the membership of TWU. The ailing Transport Workers responded in kind by increasing their activity and enlisting the support of the newly created citywide Taxi Workers' Union.[37] However, by the spring of 1947 the Transport Workers revoked the Taxi Workers' Union charter, feeling embittered that their efforts to organize the cabmen were, "like pouring money down a rat hole."[38] In the spring of 1949 Mineworkers called a strike against all fleet owned cabs in an effort to put the heat on the taxicab situation. However, Lewis's organizing efforts were thinly veiled forms of outside agitation. In fact, the fleet drivers in the city had nothing to do with the vote called in favor of the strike. *The New York Times* reported that scores of drivers both for and against the strike had said the

meeting was packed by organizers and by members of the United Mine
Workers of America. Transportation workers, mine workers, and long-
shoremen constituted three-quarters of those attending.[39] The bogus strike
vote worked to undermine Mr. Lewis's strength in the taxi industry and
drew a reaction of distrust among all drivers for the organizing activities
of outsiders, or as they were more commonly called, "labor racketeers."
Lewis's success was short lived, since much of his power over the cab driver
was based on his reputation among mine workers and the fear of violence
and personal injury which many drivers felt would arise if they crossed
paths with Lewis's organization. Coercion and intimidation obviously could
not be used to promote camaraderie among the hack profession.

Interestingly enough, as the union's efforts to ramrod a takeover of the
industry failed, the blame for the fiasco was placed upon the favorite scapegoat of the early fifties, the communists. John Lewis in one of his more
defensive moods said, "The increasing dissension within the union developed with the efforts of the Communists to move in on the UMW.[40] Despite
their failure, the Mineworkers remained involved in the taxi industry for
several years after their 1949 embarrassment.

The Teamsters:
The National Connection to Local Corruption

As early as the spring of 1949 the Teamsters renewed their efforts to
organize the hack profession.[41] Dave Beck, then president of the International Brotherhood of Teamsters, fully endorsed the organizing drive
among taxi drivers. However, little was done to strengthen the Teamsters'
control of the taxi industry until the spring of 1953. The united Automobile
Workers, in the interim, stepped in to organize.

This organization (later called the Allied Industrial Workers) is not to
be confused with Walter Reuther's United Automobile Workers, since it
had no members involved in automobile manufacturing.[42] They were strictly a racket-ridden union, run to extort monies from the drivers and the
management. Local 102 of the Auto Workers Union, like its predecessor,
run by the Mineworkers, was attempting to broaden its membership base
and had no particular interest in cab drivers. After entering the field in 1951
Local 102 spent nearly a year trying to gain control of the industry. When
all else failed, the Auto Workers called a strike as a way of disrupting the
industry and forcing an acceptance of their union.[43] This, however, was a
fruitless venture since Local 102 like nearly all previous outside agitators
found little support among the hack profession.[44]

While the chartering of a single UAW-AFL Local in New York City did not on the face of it appear to be an important national matter, this Local started a chain of events which resulted in some of the worst labor scandals in the history of the United States. In 1957 the McClellan Committee on Improper Activities in the Labor or Management Field exposed the effects of the UAW Local 102. The McClellan Committee enumerated the following consequences of the chartering of Local 102.

1. The influx of the worst types of gangsters and hoodlums into the New York labor movement.

2. The ultimate public revelation that thousands of Puerto Rican and Negro workers were exploited and subjugated through "sweetheart" contracts and deals between unscrupulous labor leaders and greedy employers.

3. The alliance between James R. Hoffa, current general president of the International Brotherhood of Teamsters, and Dioguardi, the indicted conspirator in the blinding of the labor columnist Victor Riesel.

4. The attempt, through these selfsame UAW-AFL Locals by Hoffa, in cooperation with Dio and another New York labor and narcotics racketeer, Anthony (Tony Ducks) Corallo, to rig the election of the officers of Joint Council No. 16 of the International Brotherhood of Teamsters.[45]

Since Johnny Dio was central to the New York City labor scandal unearthed by the McClellan Committee, a brief look at his background is helpful for placing the history of his operations within the taxi industry into perspective.

Born in New York in April of 1914 his criminal career blossomed while still a teenager. At the age of 18 he was arrested for coercion and conspiracy. He was acquitted on one of these charges and the other was dismissed. His criminal aspirations were bolstered by his two younger brothers who also went on to careers in crime. But it was his uncle, James Plumeri, also known as Jimmy Doyle, a notorious New York racketeer who led him to commit an act that led to arrest in 1937 when he was charged with extortion. Dio was sentenced to five years in the Sing Sing Penitentiary for his activities and shakedowns in connection with the garment industry.

After getting out of the penitentiary, he remained on the right side of the law up until his association with the UAW. After a man named Samuel Zakman, a former Communist party member, obtained the charter for Local 102 in the fall of 1950, Dio stepped into the union's affairs. The McClellan Committee unearthed the following evidence:

"On to Times Square!" shouted the strikers at City Hall, leaving in their wake fifty smashed cabs. (New York Daily News Photo)

At first he contented himself with lending money to the infant Local, while Zakman went out and started organizing some shops. In about May when the Local moved to new headquaters, Johnny Dio took over an office in the headquarters, although he had no official connection with the union. A month later, in June of 1951, Dioguardi became business manager.[46]

Interestingly enough, a new charter was issued to Local 102 in April of 1951. This charter included the name of Johnny Dioguardi which had not been included on the original charter. The new charter was granted by Anthony Doria, International secretary treasurer of the UAW-AFL and a peripheral figure in Dio's racket.

The McClellan Committee reported:

> As far as the International was concerned, Dioguardi assumed control of the Local at that time, although it seemed apparent that it took Zakman some time to find this out. Zakman testified that he noticed that Dioguardi exercised more and more authority within the Local and started adding organizers to the union staff.[47]

These organizers were strikingly effective in the New York labor movement despite their lack of experience. However, the president of the Local, Samuel Zakman, did not concur with Dio's schemes, feeling he should have more to say about who was hired as organizers. This led Zakman to resign from the union since it had become obvious to him that Dio was exercising more control as business manager than he was as president.[48]

With Zakman out of the picture, Dio began to branch out widely in the labor union movement in New York. He chartered several more Locals and became the regional director of the International Union. The Locals chartered by Dio had a common denominator—their leadership was composed of men with lengthy and unsavory police records. Dio's scheme to infiltrate the New York labor movement with gangsters of every kind was a decision which involved many other underworld characters. In particular he formed an alliance with Anthony (Tony Ducks) Corallo who exercised control over several New York unions including locals in the Teamsters, the UAW-AFL, the Retail Clerks International Association, and the United Textile Workers of America.[49] Corallo was considered to be one of the most powerful underworld figures in the New York area both in narcotics and in labor rackets. His ability to escape convictions during the thirties and forties, earned him the title "Tony Ducks."[50]

Soon after Dio became actively involved in the operation of Local 102, he turned his attention toward organizing the taxicab drivers of New York. Lester Washburn as the president of the UAW-AFL later recounted that:

Shortly after we got started in New York, this question of organizing taxicabs came up. I was opposed to that by the way. But especially in that particular organizational effort, and after learning what the history of the rackets in New York was, you could see pretty well the advantages to any underworld organization to have control of the taxicab drivers of New York. It would be a pretty powerful outfit with approximately 30,000 members, if they succeeded in organizing them.[52]

Dio's alliance with Ducks Corallo had been an effort to corral the taxi drivers as well as everybody else in New York into their local unions. However, more prominent labor leaders were involved in the plot as well. Jimmy Hoffa, then vice president of the Teamsters, developed a friendship with Johnny Dio and Ducks Corallo with the purpose of propelling his larger political ambitions within the Teamsters Union. Hoffa was aware that Dio had many connections in New York and could be an invaluable link in his bid to gain political influence in the New York area and the Teamsters as a whole. During the early fifties, Hoffa set his sights on the presidency of the Teamsters, a decision which led him to use Johnny Dio for the purpose of gaining power.

By the spring of 1953 it had become apparent to taxi drivers that Local 102 was a major blemish on the New York labor movement. Nevertheless, Johnny Dio's criminal record was the only evidence Lester Washburn could muster in support of his drive to revoke the charter of the taxicab local. He did not have sufficient evidence to oust Dio but at the insistence of George Meany, and under the threat of expulsion of the UAW from the AFL, Washburn revoked Local 102. As of June of 1953 Local 102 was defunct.[53] However, the disappearance of Local 102 led to further trouble. Soon Johnny Dio attempted to take the union charter of Local 102 and turn it over to Jimmy Hoffa and the International Brotherhood of Teamsters. This move was rapidly blocked by George Meany, president of the AFL and Tom Hickey, a vice president of the Teamsters.

Having been foiled in his attempt to walk off with the charter of Local 102, Dio secretly enlisted in the labor union network of Jimmy Hoffa, then vice president of the Teamsters. It came as more than a mere coincidence that the International Brotherhood of Teamsters formally announced intentions of organizing the hack profession in the spring of 1953.[54] On the face of it, the Teamsters' reappearance within the taxi industry after repeated failures in the early twenties, thirties and forties came as somewhat of a surprise. However, the key to the Teamsters' interest was Dio's link to Hoffa and his larger scheme of controlling the port of New York and the Eastern Seaboard.

Although the Teamsters replaced the racketeer-dominated union of Local 102, its efforts proved to be a covert continuation of Dio rule. Dio remained with the UAW until 1954 when Washburn revoked the charters to all his New York Locals. At that time Dio was serving a prison term for violation of New York State income tax laws—a violation which was an outgrowth of his interest in both sides of the "labor management street."[55] He had been Director of the UAW in New York while at the same time owning a string of cheap dress manufacturing firms. Dio was convicted for failing to report $11,200 he received in the sale of one of his firms. This amount had been paid in return for the assurance that the new owner would keep the shop non-union—as it had been under Dio.

To get Dio to leave the UAW was no simple job—it took an enormous bribe to do the trick. Anthony Doria arranged for Dio to get $16,000 upon leaving the UAW, a sum that presumably was a repayment of loans Dio had made to various Locals.[56] During this period Dio had remained an integral part of Hoffa's labor schemes in New York. In reality, his departure from the UAW little affected his relationship to the New York labor movement or his involvement with Ducks Corallo and Jimmy Hoffa. The revocation of Dio's six UAW charters in April of 1954 merely transfered those hoodlum locals into the jurisdiction of the Teamsters empire under Jimmy Hoffa.[58]

It took two and one half years before the Teamsters managed to find the time to get an intensive membership drive underway. Under Local 826 the Teamsters finally decided to, "put the heat on" by calling for a general strike in the month of January 1956. Although this represented the pinnacle of Teamsters efforts in the cab industry, the general consensus was that the strike had been a fizzle.[58]

Following the strike, the union made no demands upon the fleet owners, merely stating that the strike had been a show of strength (obviously it was not) to achieve recognition for the union. The union's position was clearly weak and its rhetoric was the only device that supported its claims as a contender for the taxi labor force.

This strike along with further exploits of Local 826 revealed the true nature of the Teamsters Local. It became increasingly obvious to the hack profession that Local 826 was a "paper local" without any members, used as part of a larger Teamsters scheme. Local 826, however, had not been created and chartered under the direction of Hoffa, since Thomas Hickey had thwarted Dio's desire to enter the taxi field in 1953. Nevertheless, Local 826 was fraught with similar union corruption and apparently was operating for the benefit of Hickey's competing faction within the Teamster organization. Although it was difficult to determine the exact relationship

Taxis bottle up traffic on express streets. (New York Daily News Photo)

Hoffa, Dio, and Corallo had to the taxi industry between 1953 and 1957, it was certainly obvious that the phony locals which had been transfered from the UAW to Hoffa's control were instrumental in his rise to power.

Hoffa's larger machinations aggravated the racketeering and extortion conducted under the Teamster's pawn, William Nuchow, president of Local 826. In March 1956 William Nuchow along with Abraham Veinstein, an official in Local 826, were arrested on charges of felonious assault when they and 50 other cab drivers assaulted a lone cabby.[61] It was a rather pathetic incident in the history of Local 826 and it pointed to the bankruptcy of power among teamster organizers. It appeared to be the last mocking gesture of the ineffectual racket-ridden Teamsters that the president of the union should personally take a hand in mugging a lone cab driver. Indeed Thomas Hickey, vice president of the parent union, seemed to give the event added weight when he protested that the police were needlessly interfering in the union organizing drive.[62]

In the summer of 1959 Local 826 made another attempt to gain control of the taxi labor force. This time Johnny Dio was behind bars and the Local was run by Frank Cassata. An arbitrated election was asked for by the Teamsters; however, this gesture of arbitration came too late. Within two weeks of their push to unionize drivers, John O'Rourke, the New York Teamster boss, was indicted for extortion in Nassau county.[64] O'Rourke along with 11 others were sent to jail on counts of extortion, coercion and conspiracy. The actual charges against the Teamster boss centered on the jukebox industry, which was being manipulated by the paper local 266, functioning exclusively for purposes of extortion and coercion of jukebox operators.

In the fall of 1960, despite heavy opposition, the Teamsters obtained the right to hold elections with 60 fleets and thereby confirm its baseless power. The time for the election was highly unfavorable for the Teamsters, since it was generally understood by drivers that the Teamsters was ready to wash its hands of the whole taxicab business. It could not have been much of a surprise that this "goon union," as it was commonly called, was soundly defeated in 57 of the 60 garages; indeed, it was rather remarkable that it actually won the right to represent one garage in light of the fact that not more than 200 drivers (a small fraction of all of New York City hacks) were dues paying members of the Teamster's Local 826.[65]

Although the Teamsters Union managed to stay in the taxi business until 1964, its efforts were limited to one garage. During this period the Landrum Griffin Act was passed, designed to curb racketeering in unions. Quite appropriately, the Teamster Local 826 became the test case in the investigations of mismanaged union funds and union fund reporting. Abraham Veinstein, former secretary-treasurer of Teamster Local 826 was indicted by a grand jury on charges of embezzling union funds, to which he pleaded guilty. This set the stage for the further probes into the racket-ridden Local 826.

The early history of labor efforts in the taxi industry was marred by the machinations of the underworld and the corruption of union politics. Union organizers within the industry continually used the taxi driver as a tool in much larger games of politics or corruption. Ironically the cab driver was never able to organize his profession because of the fact that outside organizers controlled the operations of the taxi labor force from its earliest days. The corruption of past union efforts within the industry has led the cab driver to develop a distrustful attitude toward all attempts at unionization. In part the history of corruption within past unions has promoted the driver to conceive of collective bargaining as a personal affair—an attitude that has reinforced his psychology of beating the system, and marred subsequent attempts at unionization.

Many New Yorkers prefer the gypsy cabs. The gypsy driver's slogan is the only answer to the Yellow Cab Propaganda—"Ride Yellow Ride Safe." (Photography by Paul Vidich)

5

Unionization Reconsidered

Collective Bargaining Goes Underground

Despite the fabled corruption of past efforts to unionize the drivers, another attempt was made in the early sixties. Unlike past efforts this movement developed from within the ranks of the hack profession and had the initial support of 160 taxi drivers.[1] However, the Taxi Driver Alliance, as it was called, soon found that without the support of outside organizers its efforts were doomed to failure. The virtues of an organization created and maintained by cab drivers were outweighed by the notorious independent nature of the cab driver.

After two years of indecision, this relatively informal group decided that a union was needed to counter the abuses of its bosses. In the early spring of 1964 the members of the Alliance turned to look for an established union for support in their efforts. Their first inclination was to approach the Central Labor Council which they did in May of 1964. Two representatives of the Alliance met with Harry Van Arsdale and found that he was willing to give his support.

By the end of June the Central Labor Council pledged its support to the efforts of cab drivers to form a union. However, Van Arsdale emphasized that the cab drivers would have to take the first step even though they would receive his full support. Two months later the Council voted to begin the organizing drive and launched the campaign by creating the Taxi Drivers Organizing Committee. The initial meeting of the Taxi Drivers Organizing Committee was relatively successful compared to past organizing attempts. Unlike previous efforts, this committee had the backing of some of the city's most influential labor leaders as well as the American Federation of Labor and the Congress of Industrial Organizations. Its supporters, unlike those of many previous cab unions, were labor leaders with clean records. Furthermore, the Organizing Committee was given a great deal of political support by Mayor Wagner. The Mayor made an appearance at the drivers' first meeting and blessed their efforts to unionize the industry.[2]

Politics and Unionization:
Mayor Wagner Bargains for Van Arsdale

Van Arsdale's connection to Mayor Wagner was a significant part of the success of the early union. An increase in the fare rate had been pending in the city council as early as April of 1964; however, Van Arsdale managed to delay its passage long enough to begin organizing the industry. This was accomplished through his close friendship with Mayor Wagner. The two men working together were able to promote the union's growth and create a climate in which the taxi drivers were able to gain recognition from the city's fleet owners. With Van Arsdale supported by the powerful labor leaders of the city and Mayor Wagner wielding the keys to the legal structure of the industry, the cab drivers were able to pull themselves together.

Wagner assured the initial organizers that he was totally behind them. As he stated:

> We want to make sure when the legislation is passed—which I hope will be soon—that the benefits go to the drivers and not to the coffers of the fleet owners.[3]

The fare rise was passed at the end of September of 1964. Van Arsdale would have preferred to stall longer but political pressures from the fleet owners were too much. Potentially the passage of the cab fare bill could have been a major blow to the strength of the taxi drivers; like times in the past it was felt that fleet owners were attempting to thwart the creation of a union by increasing fares and increasing drivers' income. However, the quick passage of the cab fare bill did not kill the organizing drive.

Instead of attempting to organize the industry all at once, as many other unions had tried in the past, the Organizing Committee began working with only those garages that had expressed an interest. Within six months of its initial drive, the Organizing Committee had obtained 18,000 signatures authorizing the Taxi Driver Organizing Committee as its bargaining agent.

By February of 1965 the Taxi Drivers' Organizing Committee (TDOC) had begun to get some momentum. This was reflected in the increased use of coercion and intimidation by the fleet owners. The owners turned to any and all measures to undercut the growth of the union since it was becoming obvious that Van Arsdale was not about to give up the fight. The Metropolitan Taxi Board of Trade, acting as lobbyists for the fleet owners, actively solicited additional part-time drivers in an effort to dilute the strength of Van Arsdale's followers.[4] These men were hired by the fleet owner as a reserve pool in case the regular drivers were to call a strike. In this way the owner could counter the threat of a strike with a labor force batting for his team.[5]

On March 24, 1965 Van Arsdale called a one day general strike to show his strength.[6] It was a relatively effective strike; however, it was marred by several minor skirmishes between Van Arsdale's electrical workers and drivers who refused to participate in the strike. This was the first major strike to hit New York since the Mineworkers halted cabs for nine days in 1949.

One month after the strike, a newly created Wagner Taxicab Panel recommended that the N.L.R.B. be given jurisdiction over the dispute. The panel indicated that a citywide election was preferable to one conducted on an individual garage basis, since it would promote stability within the industry. An all or nothing confrontation inevitably worked to favor the union in its goal of total bargaining power over all fleet operations.[7] Furthermore, the other critical issue discussed by the Wagner panel was whether part-timers would be allowed to vote in the election. Fleet owners naturally favored the idea that all drivers should be given the right to vote, whereas the union believed the moonlighters within the industry should be separated from the regular drivers in determining voting standards.

Van Arsdale Gains Control

On June 28 the union called for another citywide strike to publicize their efforts. The pressure was directed at the NLRB since Van Arsdale was concerned with setting an election date. Unlike previous strikes, this one lasted seven days and was quite effective in stalling cab service throughout the city. Moreover, the strike secured its purpose of setting an election date for the industry. On June 29 the NLRB set July 21, 1965 as the election date for 38 garages throughout the city. The NLRB ruled that the election would be held in individual garages rather than on a citywide basis, which was somewhat of a blow to the union. However, this setback was compensated by the NLRB decision setting new eligibility standards for the industry. Rather than allowing all drivers to vote, they indicated that only drivers who had worked a total of 26 days in the three month period immediately preceding the election would be eligible to vote.

The NLRB election ruling did not stop the striking cab drivers. In fact, the strike became more violent in the following days. The police reported as many as 130 separate incidents which were marked by violence, threats of assault, and damage to taxicabs. Some of the blame for the violence was put on the fleet owners for stalling off their recognition of the union. As Paul O'Dwyer, councilman at large, stated:

> The refusal of the fleet owners to engage in civilized collective bargaining has created an atmosphere in this city conducive to violence and is causing substantial inconvenience to the public.[8]

The fleet owners appeared to be in a relatively favorable position. They had chosen the garages that they felt had the greatest number of part-time drivers as well as those who appeared most likely to vote against Van Arsdale. Their emphasis was on dividing the strength of the union and creating a bogus set of choices. As a result, the fleet owners promoted the paper local 826 of the Teamsters, despite Van Arsdale's protests, to be entered on the ballot.[9] Although Local 826 had been operating in the city since 1953, in the early sixties it had existed without the support of the Joint Council of 16 or the parent union run by Jimmy Hoffa. Its presence on the July 21 ballot was less an indication of Teamster support for the industry than a tactic used by the fleet owner to split the drivers' votes and narrow the success of the Taxi Organizing Committee. However, these tactical ploys all failed on July 21 when the TDOC won the right to represent 22 of the 37 garages involved in the election.[10] Only one garage voted against the union and 14 other garages were challenged by the fleet owner to stall off the eventual certification of Van Arsdale's union. Overall, the Taxi Drivers Organizing Committee got 64 percent of all the votes, the Teamsters got four percent, and 32 percent of the drivers voted for no union at all.

The second skirmish with the fleet owners came on December 21, 1965 when the 43 remaining taxi garages voted under NLRB supervision. Once again, the TDOC did convincingly well. They won in 28 garages, losing in only one and were challenged by the owners in the 14 remaining garages. However, it took until April of 1966 before the TDOC was certified as the representative of 29 of the 43 garages involved in the December election. Eventually the challenged ballots were awarded to the TDOC and Van Arsdale's union was given a definite victory in 78 of the 80 garages that had submitted to the election.

Collective Bargaining: The City Settles the Issue

On May 11, 1966 the Union initiated another strike lasting for six days in the hope of forcing an increase in their commissions and other benefits. Van Arsdale demanded that commissions be increased from the 45 percent then being offered to 50 percent of the total. Fleet owners were unwilling to offer that much of the pie to the driver. However, the fleet owners agreed to let Mayor Lindsay settle the dispute after they reached a stalemate in their negotiations with the union. Mr. Lindsay formulated an 18 month contract that provided a 46 percent commission for all drivers and called for an increase of one percent after December of 1966. All drivers working 60 days during a three month period were eligible for an additional one percent bonus.

The mayor was rather irritated that the two-year drive to win collective bargaining rights resulted in the city settling the dispute. As Mr. Lindsay stated:

> It is understandable that a first contract in so large an industry, involving so many thousands and thousands of employees, is most difficult to negotiate, but it is also disappointing that true collective bargaining between the parties could not bring about collective bargaining agreement.[11]

The owners' uncooperativeness extended beyond the sphere of union recognition. At first, the owners were even unwilling to let the union incorporate the part-timers into their ranks, since part-timers had not been allowed to vote for the union. However, the owners' position was simply an extension of their desire to continue undermining the strength of Van Arsdale's efforts. Because of the stalemate, Mr. Lindsay finally stepped in and decreed that all cab drivers fell under the jurisdiction of the union.

As the 18 month contract was coming to a close, owners and union officials were unable to agree on a new contract. The chief problem of the negotiations was reluctance of the owners to increase the drivers' wages without assurances that the city would raise the fares to absorb some of the costs. Van Arsdale was asking for an increase in commissions totalling 52 percent of the meter and fleet owners were reluctant to absorb the costs all by themselves. They felt that a 47 percent commission was reasonable and tried to convince the union that a fare increase by itself would benefit drivers and owners alike without the need for an increase in the commission rate. The owners in truth were extremely hesitant to part with any of their share of the "take." They were all too aware that the three percent increase in commissions had cost them over 7.5 million dollars under one year of Van Arsdale's contract.

The crisis was compounded by Mayor Lindsay's belief that the industry should settle on contract terms before the city would consider raising the fares. This left the fleet owners in a position of passing a wage increase on to the driver without being certain Mayor Lindsay would actually consider raising the fares. Negotiations were brought to a halt at the termination of the old contract on November 16, 1967, as unsanctioned sporadic striking broke out throughout the city. Van Arsdale had asked the drivers to postpone the strike, at the request of the mayor. However, the independent-minded drivers ignored his plea. His strength as the boss of the union was being severely tested and Van Arsdale was not able to keep them in line. Wildcat strikes continued for nearly ten days despite Van Arsdale's pleas that the drivers return to work so that negotiations could continue. The old labor leader was beginning to understand why all the other organizing efforts of the past century had ended in defeat. Perhaps he was beginning to realize that his victory speech of 1965 had been too optimistic.

At a union meeting on November 21, Van Arsdale addressed the issue of continued negotiations.[12] Most of the drivers were eager to open up the strike and shut down all cab service, but Van Arsdale was opposed to this measure. He asked all drivers to stand up if they favored continued negotiations, and only one-third of the 3,000 drivers got to their feet. Realizing the drivers' opposition, Van Arsdale conveniently omitted to ask for an opposing vote and publicly concluded that the majority were in favor of more negotiations. Many of the drivers were irritated with this tactic and felt mocked by Van Arsdale; they proceeded to boo his speech and shout accusations of "dictator" to the stage. For the driver it was a simple issue regardless of how complicated Van Arsdale wished to make it. Throughout Van Arsdale's recital of union accomplishments, shouts of "money" were made by many of the drivers. They didn't care about the abstract issues of benefits and pension funds; all they wanted was a grab on the money, a pastime at which they were well versed.

On the 24th of November the owners and union reached an agreement, with a little help from Mayor Lindsay. A three-year contract was approved contingent on the passage of a fare increase for the entire industry. The contract provided for a 48 percent commission rate for the first 18 months, to be followed by a 49 per cent commission thereafter. Moreover, those drivers who had worked full time for ten years or more were offered a 49 percent commission to be followed by a 1 percent raise. This agreement was the first step in reinforcing the traditional caste system that has long existed between full-time drivers and part-timers within the industry. However, the marginal difference in pay rates was not enough to divide the hack profession on the value of the contract. They approved it by a three to one majority.

On January 16, 1968 a 30 percent increase in cab fares was passed by the city council. Their decision had been spurred on by a one-day strike involving most of the city's taxis. Despite their agreement, the fleet owners were unhappy with the increase. It was their contention that the new fare rate structure would necessitate an increase in fares within a year. This, however, did not occur.

Inability to Create a Closed Shop

Instead the owners embarked upon a major campaign to hire new drivers, which has had disastrous consequences for the apparently strong taxicab union. The implication of this action has been that the union membership card is no more than a required ticket stub permitting entrance to any person possessing a hack license. Any and all drivers over the age of 19 capable of passing a police department security check are eligible to obtain this license.

It has not always been so easy to become a cab driver in New York. Prior to 1969 the police department had an application procedure that weeded out nearly everybody who applied.[13] The fleet owners were rather perturbed by the police department's inefficiency in processing applicants and were critical of the overly difficult geography test administered to the inexperienced drivers. The owners were all too aware that a constant supply of new applicants was their only assurance that business would continue as usual despite the union's efforts to create a closed shop. Without this assurance, the fleet owners felt that the high turnover of the labor force would bring the taxi industry to a grinding halt. In the spring of 1969, at the request of the fleet owners, the police department simplified their geography test and allowed the Metropolitan Taxi Board of Trade to initiate its own temporary licensing program to pick up the slack in police processing procedures. The effect of this reform was that an applicant could get a hack license in two to three days, rather than the two or three months it took with the police. The geography test also became so simple that an out-of-towner could pass it without setting foot in Manhattan.[14]

Within two years of the institution of temporary licensing procedures, the fleet owners had processed over 40,000 applicants. In addition, the normal application procedure continued to function. By 1971 there were as many as 90,000 eligible taxi drivers in the city of New York;[15] nearly one out of every 100 New Yorkers had become a licensed cab driver.

The union has been sharply opposed to the owners' insistence on issuing an excessive number of hack licenses. From their standpoint, an oversupply of drivers limits their ability to create a closed shop agreement with fleet owners and prompts the industry to accept a transient and unpredictable work force as the backbone of its operations. Instead of making the job intrinsically worthwhile, the union feels it has remained what it always has been and conceivably always will be—a form of unemployment insurance for New Yorkers.

There are good reasons why cab driving has been such a popular choice of occupations for the recent college graduates and the unemployed. The average cab driver working five days a week on a 49 percent commission makes about $175 a week including tips. There are many drivers who make sums vastly exceeding this amount. As one driver said:

> Now you take the owner drivers, they do very, very well. There's no doubt in my mind an owner driver can net, and I'm talking net not gross, 300 to 350 a week. In fact I know owner drivers that gross over 100 dollars a day, six days a week. But they're workers.

> VIDICH: What's the most a fleet driver can make?

> AL: I know drivers who in the old days used to make 300 dollars a week. The hustlers, the cheaters—the guys that played the airports to a fair thee well.

However most cabbies doing arm jobs or working the cab for nine or ten hours a day, five days a week usually make 200 or 225 a week. To make alot of money requires a lot of time and patience and many cabbies are not interested in working hard partly because they have no great commitment to their work. Undoubtedly the presence of many undependable and un-motivated workers in the industry has been a result of the ease with which a hack license can be obtained. The ease with which a hack license can be obtained has had its consequences.

Although there are only 6,816 fleet taxis, there is no fleet in the entire city which has been able to operate all of its cabs all of the time, 90,000 hack licenses notwithstanding. Despite the fact that fleet owners will overstock their roster with as many as six men available for each cab, the industry is unable to fully operate all of its vehicles. In effect, by excessively stockpiling their labor supply, the bosses have devalued the profession.

The low status of the profession can clearly be seen by correlating the number of eligible cab drivers with the unemployment trends in the larger national economy. As the number of jobs available throughout other sectors of the economy become more scarce, hack licenses tend to increase in number. As the following graph shows, during the depression in the thirties, as well as the recent recession under the Nixon administration, the number of hack licenses issued has increased with rising unemployment.[16] This correlation was most apparent prior to the emergence of the present union, since recent collective bargaining efforts have increased the desirability of obtaining a license.

The open door into the hack profession denies it status and respectability. The temporary nature of most of the fleet owner's work force has turned the hope of a stable profession into a vicious circle. Allowing the present breed of drivers to operate taxis entails a perpetuation of the status of the profession, and yet attempts to limit the work force are feared to be threats to the full operation of the taxi fleets.

The nature of the taxi industry has changed little over the past 50 years. During the 1930s the same situation existed that presently plagues the union, i.e., an oversupply of labor. The report of the Mayor's Committee on Taxicab Survey under Mayor La Guardia aptly described the problem:

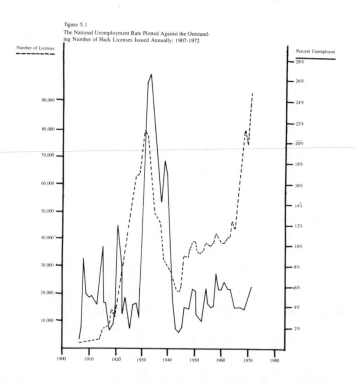

figure 5.1
The National Unemployment Rate Plotted Against the Outstanding Number of Hack Licenses Issued Annually: 1907-1972

The condition of the driver in the industry, whether he works for a fleet or is an owner driver is deplorable. . . . The situation might very well exist due to the depression and the excessive number of cabs even if there were a reasonable supply of drivers available, but exploitation of the driver is made easier and his distress intensified by the fact that there is a tremendous excess in the number of licensed drivers.[17]

Nothing has changed since the date Mayor La Guardia read the above statement. In fact the situation has worsened, since there are now 90,000 outstanding licenses whereas there were only 58,000 in 1934 at the time of the taxicab survey. There have never been more eligible drivers in the industry than at the present time. Not even the 80,000 hacks licensed during the peak of the depression in 1931, exceed the total of 90,000 in 1971.

The union, taking a back seat in the labor problems of the industry, knows full well that its power is forever limited without a closed shop within the industry. Union members have insisted to no avail that the number of licenses be limited to no more than 40,000 to 45,000 outstanding. Without a strong inner core of committed drivers the union is at the mercy of the fleet owners and must depend during times of crisis upon Van Arsdale's electrical workers to swing union strength. It has been the hope of Local 3036 to build a stable brotherhood, self-supporting in battle with the fleet owners. However this has not been possible nor is it an apt description of the labor history of the present local. The International Brotherhood of Electrical Workers was the catalyst behind much of the early unionizing drive because Van Arsdale was able to enlist its support and use its energy to organize an otherwise disinterested taxi labor force. When strength on the picket line or in the union meeting was lacking, Van Arsdale could rely on his power in the New York IBEW to influence decisions in a manner he felt appropriate to the best interests of the taxi driver.

With these forms of coercion Van Arsdale has been able to separate his power from the power, or lack of it, belonging to the 90,000 potential cab drivers. By developing an independent base of support outside of the taxi work force and with a modicum of support from within, he has been able to hold control of the union for ten years; an unusual achievement in an industry that resisted unionization for over 57 years.

The fleet owners are not totally responsible for exploiting an oversupply of labor; they have had the tacit support of the police department and now of the Taxi and Limousine Commission. The police department, since it took over control of the industry in 1925, has done nothing to develop a sound labor force.

In fact the main purpose for police regulation of the industry was to eliminate the criminal element, that had infiltrated the profession during the early twenties. Nevertheless, during the 46 years the industry was under the supervision of the police department's hack bureau, not a single attempt was made to improve the work force of the industry. No new programs for attracting better qualified applicants or more permanent workers was conceived. Rather than attempting to plan for better working conditions, better services, and a reasonable return to the owners, the police acquiesced to the will of the large fleet owners. As a result, the regulatory authorities have found themselves taking sides with the vested interests of the fleet owner who has sought to maintain high levels of operation rather than relative stability to the work force. The police department ignored the need for planning within the industry by confusing licensing with regulation. The emphasis was placed upon the criminal record of the applicant rather than his employment history. The same policy has been continued to a somewhat lesser degree by the police department's successor, the Taxi and Limousine Commission.

The Union Sells Out

The industry, as usual, reached another stalemate at the termination of its third contract. In the fall of 1970 the industry found itself dealing simultaneously with a wage and fare increase. In effect, the public at large was beginning to realize that it was paying for the additional costs of union contracts. The owners, as in the previous contract, were unwilling to bargain with the union on its own terms. Rather, they wanted to pass the burden of the contract on to the city council and the taxi-riding public. Their policy was a clever means of avoiding cost efficiency in the face of union negotiations. After 15 days of striking in December of 1970, the union hierarchy agreed to a contract with the fleet owners. In order to get the drivers' approval to end the strike, Van Arsdale called a mass meeting on December 20, 1971.[18] Many drivers were eager to call a halt to the strike, since two weeks without work had severely affected their finances. However, many drivers charged that Van Arsdale had packed the meeting with electrical workers to assure a favorable reaction to his new contract with the fleet owners. Young drivers, in particular, were the most irritated with his "deal" with the bosses, since it denied benefits to the part-timer and reduced the commission of all new drivers.

The strike was settled although few drivers were really satisfied with the agreement. The new contract called for a drastic reduction in the commission rate offered to new drivers, and it provided that a dime off each initial drop of the meter would go to improved pensions, holidays and sick benefits for the full-time workers. The contract smacked of a sellout and nobody was thoroughly happy. New drivers were to receive 42 percent of the meter and be eligible for a 2 percent boost every 200 days of work until their commission was 50 percent. The old drivers would maintain their 49 or 50 percent commission as usual; however they would pay a dime on each trip to the union pension fund. Everybody had a gripe with the new contract. In fact the dissent became so great, the contract was never ratified by the membership even though the fleet owners put it into operation.

From December of 1970 to December of 1972 the industry operated without a ratified contract or a functioning union. During this time drivers paid dues and received a reduced commission while the union made no efforts to renegotiate a tenable agreement with the fleet owners. It was the opinion of most drivers that Local 3036 was top-heavy with corruption like all of the rest of the organizing drives of the past, because the fleet owners had sabotaged its strength and union racketeers were busy cashing in on the workers condition. As one disenchanted and dissident shop chairman stated in the fall of 1973, "there have been no garage meetings in over two years. Van Arsdale has people to make sure the membership does not attend. Of course the owners are doing their job." In addition, cabbies have been adamant in denouncing Harry Van Arsdale's manner of conducting those meetings that do take place. One driver said, "Whenever he (Van Arsdale) sees that his meetings are jammed, he's democratic. Otherwise he is not. Definitely he is not. At times you definitely have to look around to see who's behind you. It's like a real nazified meeting."

During the four years since Van Arsdale was re-elected to the presidency of the union he has used the abstract principles of union democracy and worker participation in leadership as a means of hiding what is an unabashed dictatorship. The union has initiated a procedure of asking the drivers what they want done—a clever means of making their racketeering look more respectable. The real effect of this procedure has been to dissolve true leadership and maintain the union racketeers in a position of power. As one driver stated:

> "They ask the drivers what they want. If you were to ask why they dont lead the men they cop out by saying, 'but isn't this the best way of doing things?' Of course the union has its answer for everything. This is what they call leadership—practically abdicated in a sense."

In response to continued wildcat strikes throughout 1972, protesting the 42 percent commission, the union finally agreed to have the situation arbitrated by the state mediation board. On December 27, 1972 the union and the fleet owners agreed to a new contract, which was little different than the previous one. Van Arsdale agreed to a 43 percent commission in place of the 42 percent commission and somehow most drivers present at the April meeting in 1973 were satisfied with this agreement even though it was little more than a crumb. The leading opponent of Van Arsdale, Leo Lazarus, head of the Rank and File Coalition, reacted to this situation by reflecting:

> "Harry Van Arsdale had said that 42 percent was in opposition to everything we stood for. Not even 48 percent was good enough. However, when we went to binding arbitration it went from 42 to 43 percent. Harry Van Arsdale is the best organizer the fleet owners ever had."

Perhaps the only radical and conceivably lethal outgrowth of the 43 percent contract was that it established a dues checkoff system. Instead of having to go to the union every time dues are to be paid, the new system allows the fleet owner the right to deduct the dues directly out of the driver's paycheck. Although this may appear to be an improvement for some drivers who dont like to pay dues, it tends to strengthen the unchecked power of the union racketeers. As one older driver told it, "I'm not against a union getting powerful—but not under sellout conditions or bureaucratic conditions." These remarks take on a certain poignancy when they are linked to recent schemes to increase dues without increasing benefits. Although Van Arsdale has not yet publically announced that he desires to raise the dues payments, reliable sources have told the author that this event is imminent. Van Arsdale is claiming, "we dont have any money" and is expecting his cabbies to believe him.

Although most drivers have responded to union corruption in their traditional style of apathy, saying, "what the hell is the difference," a young dissident organization called the Rank and File Coalition emerged in the spring of 1972 enthused with the idea of ousting Van Arsdale and his corrupt leadership. Their arrival within the industry was in response to a new phase of the traditional problem of beating the system. Historically the owners were considered the greatest threat to all collective bargaining hopes since they were able to manipulate a disorganized hack labor force at their whim. With the entrenchment of Van Arsdale's power in the taxi industry, the union and the fleet owners have virtually merged into one corporate entity. As a consequence, the latest union sentiment of the rank and file bears a close resemblance to the traditional opinion drivers have had of the bosses. The *Hot Seat*, the monthly paper of the Taxi Rank and File Coalition expressed this problem in the fall of 1973 stating:

"In the past the union has been able to manipulate us, because we were disorganized. In the strike three years ago they were able to call off the strike without getting what we wanted. But if we can unite, then they wont be able to do that this year."[19]

Although an appallingly low number of drivers are actually satisfied with the present union or the present contract, the drivers have not responded in a collective way to the problems of union corruption. Rather they tend to revert to the neurotic pattern of "riding the arm" or hustling as the resolution of their dilemma. This behavior has been seen by the Rank and File Coalition as a so-called justification for why the, "lousy contract has been able to persist so long." The *Hot Seat* emphasized:

"Because we have such a lousy contract, people have become dependent on riding the arm to maintain their incomes. But it's hard to defend an income based on arm jobs, unlike a contract which guarantees decent wages."[20]

In light of their strong belief in the need to ride the arm, the taxi drivers of New York are in an outrage over Van Arsdale's recent agreement to employ union personnel to assist the fleet owner in catching cheating drivers. Instead of offering job protection for the cabbies this new union policy unequivocally shows that the union leaders have become a branch of the fleet owner's rat squad. "Who knows what they'll agree to next time," is the general consensus of the hack profession.

Union Meetings: Hack Politics

Although the Rank and File Coalition so far has been unsuccessful in dethroning Van Arsdale and installing itself in leadership, its efforts to do so revealed the politics and rhetoric by which the associates of Van Arsdale were successful in dividing and conquering their opponents.

It was apparent to many drivers that the election of November 1970 was rigged and the ratification of contracts and settlement of strikes arrived at in mass union meetings involved nothing more than stuffing the auditorium with Van Arsdale's other union members in the electrical trade. The backroom deals of the union hierarchy along with such events as stuffing the ballot box and masquerading electrical workers as hacks at union meeting were known to exist by most of the membership. Nevertheless, despite the overwhelming fact that many drivers were aware of Van Arsdale's political deals and somewhat dubious means of reaching his ends, the drivers were quite clearly unable to contend with his power and political acumen. In the face of obvious deception and fraud, Van Arsdale managed to win his re-election to office in November of 1971. This was accomplished through the skill of his associates in confusing the issues, refusing to answer the serious questions, and dividing the members against themselves. During the larger part of 1971 Van Arsdale's associates roamed through all of the major fleets in the city explaining the situation to the membership; or as they said, "to make the men realize that there really isn't any issue at all." The union leadership built their union meetings on the assumption that, "if you tell part of the truth but tell it well the drivers would have no grounds to stand on." Union shop chairmen and longstanding leaders of the union glorified the history of the union, berating the fleet owner, the gypsy drivers, and whoever else might charge the emotional bank of union camaraderie. Circuitous monologues and creative forms of obfuscation were liberally applied to put the men to sleep. Indeed the union leaders knew that the true test of their success was if they could walk out at the end of the meeting without the drivers knowing, "what the hell they had really said." Political rhetoric of this kind is, in all truth, not too difficult to employ in the company of hackmen who are notoriously deaf to anybody but themselves. To an extent, the union's success in avoiding the issues that many of the drivers wished to raise was handled by allowing everybody to speak so that no one was heard. Efforts to quell dissent among their ranks were dealt with by saying, "you're out of line." This was often followed by such disclaimers as, "Let's give someone else a chance to talk." These verbal prongs served to stimulate the men to react more vehemently. Nevertheless in their eager- ness to pounce on the union leaders, they failed to see the chaos created by 100 people speaking at once. Under the duress of this chaos the leaders felt quite sure older drivers would consent to nominal forms of decorum. It became quite simple to interject reasonable behavior that reflected the respectability of the leadership. "Wait until the end of the meeting to ask questions," or "you're trying to destroy the union," became the turning points in the leaders' twist to the discussion. Tumult, uproar, and the deaf ears of screaming drivers put the leaders on top. "We can only answer one at a time," whispered loudly was enough of an excuse, for the record, why the men failed to listen to their leadership. By the time the meeting had begun, it was nearly over. The anger and passion of the men was easily shunted over to a less political moment when personal dialogue would straighten out a driver's confusion. "Watch your language, you're in the company of a lady," quite appropriately signalled the end of the meeting, whereupon the leaders would say, "We'll respond to all of your questions after the meeting without taking up the time of all you who are waiting to take out a cab." The formal ending of the meeting relieved the tension and gave the drivers a chance to talk to their leaders. Or did it? The moment the obvious chaos of the meeting was brought to a halt, the drivers no longer existed as a group but fell back into their normal conflicts, agreeing on nothing more than personal issues. At election time in November of 1971, it was quite obvious Van Arsdale's men had explained where they stood. "We stand where we have always stood, behind you men," was the leaders' response.

Union Corruption: The Strength of Organized Management

Part of the reason for the general disinterest in supporting the union and improving the image of the profession is due to the nature of the union's membership. As many as 50 percent of all cab drivers are part-time workers.[21] This is a consequence of the fact that fleet owners depend upon a high volume of part-time workers to stabilize their work force and maintain a high operational level for their cabs. For the union, however, this creates a serious danger since it is left with the problem of trying to consolidate and stabilize a membership which is concerned with nothing more than temporary employment.

The fringe benefits and added commissions that the union works to obtain are almost secondary considerations to the part-time driver. The part-timer is not looking for job security or for pension plan programs, since his interest in the job and the profession is temporary. The union, confronted with this disloyal or disinterested part-time membership can not afford to rest too much of its power with these men. To do so would inevitably lead to ruin. Furthermore, the union leaders are well aware that most part-timers have no quarrel with the union since these drivers will rarely entertain the idea of hacking as a permanent career.

The union has found itself quite able to disregard the existence of the part-timer and allocate his benefits to the full-time worker. In effect, the union's position has become: "full-time drivers will get full-time benefits and part-time drivers are without benefits at all." This position strengthens the union insofar as it takes advantage of the subtle distinction existing between the full-time drivers and the part-time drivers. However, by giving the full-timer the benefits of the part-timer, the union has allied itself with only half of its workers. Unquestionably the union has gained strength, but it has done so at the expense of truly representing the vested interests of all drivers. This alliance with the older full-time drivers can only work as long as the part-timer represents no threat to the union's power.

One of the underlying causes for the lack of proportional benefits allotted to the part-timer stems from the ease with which union dues and pension

funds can be misused. As long as the part-time driver is excluded from
fringe benefits, the union can maintain authority over much greater sums
of money than are truly within their rights to demand. Enormous sums of
dues monies extracted from the part-time membership are controlled by the
union organization. These dues, in fact, never return as benefits to the
membership paying them. Rather, the money is diverted into the full-time
drivers' pension fund and sick benefit fund or passed directly into the
pockets of union officials. This latter possibility appears quite plausible at
the moment in light of the pension fund created under Van Arsdale's
unratified 1970 contract. As of December of 1972, millions of dollars
had been diverted directly into the union's pension fund established under
a contract that had not even been ratified by the union membership. Above
and beyond the practice of mismanaging union pension funds is a greater
problem of mismanaged dues payments. Full-time drivers pay $7 every two
months in dues and part-timers pay $5 over the same period. The union
claims to have, at most, 36,000 drivers under its banner; however, these
36,000 drivers are constantly changing, dropping out of the industry for
several months, returning at their whim or not returning at all. Consequently as many as 70,000 or 80,000 drivers are actually employed within the taxi
industry during any given year just to maintain a stable 36,000 working
membership. This enormous membership has poured millions of dollars
into the coffers of the union. Several million dollars annually are paid in
dues to Van Arsdale's union without anyone really knowing where it has
all gone.

The union has suffered for its unwillingness to incorporate these casual
drivers into its ranks. By totally alienating them from the benefits of the
union, they have allowed the owner access to a large pool of scab labor.
During strikes part-timers have been easily wooed into breaking strike
efforts and working for the boss. For the part-timer, his immediate need for
making a few dollars has frequently undermined successful taxi strikes.
Collective action and united strike efforts have failed in the taxi industry
because more than half of the labor force is without commitment to the
ideals of labor.

Collective Bargaining Goes Underground: The Cheaters Take Over

The breakdown in union honesty has created more than mere distrust for
the operations of Van Arsdale's union; it has pushed the driver into a
stronger belief in the need for cheating. Nearly half of all the fleet drivers
in New York justify their need to cheat because of the failure of all past
unions to meet their needs. Although this problem has been an intrinsic part

of the industry since its inception, it has gotten much worse under the lowered commission rate.

For an honest man the taxi industry has never been a profitable venture. Over the last 65 years drivers have consistently received the beggar's share of the spoils, leaving the lion's share for the bosses. This problem has been the key to the instability of the taxi labor force and has dampened most young men's career aspirations to be taxi drivers. There is no money to be made in the taxi industry for those who work honestly and little chance of a promising future for a young man looking for a career. Those who do end up as cab drivers are rarely satisfied with the wages. Moreover, their skills usually leave them few other occupational alternatives. In short, there is little or no job satisfaction and virtually no sense of self-purpose above and beyond the need to survive. Furthermore, the nature of taxi driving makes it very difficult to value one's work since the sole purpose of becoming a cab driver is cruising the streets to make a buck.

Inevitably the lack of job satisfaction has affected the nature of the taxi industry and the strength of the taxi unions. Since drivers are unable to value their own work, they are unwilling to value the work of other cab drivers and consequently lack a genuine sense of camaraderie. As explained earlier, their aspirations are not directed towards their jobs in the sense of fulfilling a larger mission or "calling" but are geared toward taking as much as they can get without getting caught. Tragic though it is, the cab driver has systematically defeated and undermined the strength of collective bargaining for lack of a larger purpose and of a strong sense of self-worth and self-dignity. Most drivers, sadly enough, are motivated by no more than the desire to steal as much money as they can without giving anything in return to strengthen the union or the welfare of the profession.

Cheating within the context of the driver's life is an unorganized racket. Perhaps in another line of business dishonesty can be organized and the collusion can achieve a fair degree of brotherhood as in the case of the Mafia. However, in the taxi industry every cabby is literally in competition with every other cabby to make his living off the street. Drivers fight with each other to get a fare, to get the best position on the street, and to get the best place on a hack line. For this reason, there is precious little support for one driver who wants to be friendly with another.

The focus on individual action as expressed through the act of cheating has made it very difficult for the cabby to conceive of group action or union efforts. In fact, the cab driver has a strong tendency to distrust group action and group efforts, looking at them as possible "deals" or "conspiracies." However, the hacks' distrust of union action and collective effort is not unfounded. The history of past unions has done much to reinforce their lack of confidence in collective action; unfortunately, this in turn has reinforced their willingness to cheat on the boss. The driver's personal inclinations to cheat so as to rectify the inequities of the meter contract has significantly reduced the function of the union. There is no need for a union contract and all its benefits if the driver is capable of achieving all of his economic desires through personal action. For most drivers union contracts provide only a minimum wage. The rest he gains by cheating and hustling. In this sense the contract loses much of its significance, since the hack knows that wage disputes with the boss can always be resolved by dismantling the meter or riding with the flag up. The driver's own "non-union" method of negotiation with the fleet owner allows him to create a wage contract that imposes few restrictions.

This situation leaves Local 3036 with little driver support. The drivers are content to let the union go its separate way as long as it doesn't interfere with their ability to cheat and make a reasonable income. At most, the drivers expect a reasonable meter contract since they realize that the less they cheat to make a living, the less chance there is of getting caught. Because of this fear of being caught by the boss, the 42 and 43 percent contracts did not please anyone. It has meant that the driver has increased the amount of time he drives with the flag up, making money for himself while sizably increasing his chances of getting caught. For most drivers the last few years of working under "sellout contracts" has dissolved their confidence in the union, but, ironically, this has driven them *further* into their cheating philosophy. Now more than ever they are saying, "You've got to cheat to make a living in this business." However, in this case they are no longer just cheating on the boss and the passenger, but on the union contract as well.

Because of the driver's lack of confidence in the union, the taxicab union has been unable to be thoroughly effective in bargaining. The strike power of the union becomes ineffectual when drivers refuse to cooperate with the union leaders. This leaves the owners in a most advantageous position since they know that if they hold out long enough, all the drivers will return to work and forget the union efforts. Interestingly enough, in every major strike called by Van Arsdale's union, scores of cab drivers have sabotaged the effectiveness of collective action by illegally operating private automobiles as taxicabs. There is little the union can do for the cab drivers if some want to operate as scabs during strikes. What the hack is really saying by this form of action is, "I like the *idea* of making money as long as it doesn't interfere with my ability to make more money right now."

To add to the union's problems, not to mention those of the fleet owners, the gypsy cab drivers are ready and willing to take over the medallion taxicab market in the event a strike is called. During the last two major strikes in New York, the gypsies have stepped in and taken over much of the business otherwise served by the medallion cabs.[22] Their competition and their numerical strength have weakened the union's ability to negotiate effectively. In the face of a general strike, the union is all too aware that the gypsies would be ready to serve their territories of the city. Furthermore, there is a general understanding that taxi drivers would quickly switch to driving gypsy cabs if they saw the gypsy operators taking over the city. In a battle of this kind, the union would inevitably lose. The passengers would forsake the medallioned taxi and the drivers would forsake the union and the medallion industry.

Although it is the low wages which prompts many drivers to cheat in the first place, the cheating itself also causes the wages to be low. It is a circle of despair that has robbed the union of strength and the hack profession of self-respect.

6

Economics Of The Industry

Deterioration Of Public Service

During the years 1950 to 1972, while the driver suffered for lack of an honest union, the owners of the industry were developing their control over public service. The history of efforts to unionize the driver during this period was quite bitter. However, for the fleet owner the total ineffectivenesss of organized labor established and consolidated his power. In effect, the fleet was neither accountable to municipal government nor limited by the terms of collective bargaining. His economic power over the public as well as the driver has had unfortunate repercussions upon the quality and quantity of taxi service in New York. With the growing value of the government cartel established by the city council in 1937 the fleet owners lost sight of the public's interest. Their interest turned to exploiting the government sanctioned monopoly rather than meeting the needs of the city and its changing urban population.

Rise and Decline of Owner Monopoly:
Role of the Medallion

Both the owner driver and fleet medallions continued to grow in value after the fare hike of 1952. For the fleet owner, in particular, the corporate armor protecting his medallion, sparked the growth of a massive fortune. By the end of 1959 the aggregate value of all fleet owned medallions was over 135 million dollars; a dramatic increase over the $84,300 it cost the fleet owners for the original $10 licensing. The black market sale of medallions became a thriving business during the decade of the sixties. Major New York banks like the Chase Manhattan were willing to underwrite massive loans to the industry when they saw the profit potential of the medallion monopoly. The ease of obtaining bank loans as well as the increasing demand for service boosted the value of fleet medallions to their highest ever in the fall of 1964. At this point individual fleet medallions were valued at $35,000[1] and the aggregate value of all fleet owned medallions soared to $240,000,000.

The value of the medallion in effect has measured the capitalized value of the annual monopoly profits of a taxicab; in other words, you're not going to pay more for the license than you think you can get back by operating that taxi. Moreover, the value of the New York City taxi industry's monopoly has increased over time with the increase in the need for service and the increases in the cost of the service. The total value of all medallions, as a result, has reflected the monopoly value of the industry as a whole. Naturally the value of the monopoly has varied over the years. However, at its peak in 1964, the medallion franchise for fleet and owner driven taxis was worth 365 million on the black market; approximately 240 million for fleet cabs and 125 million for all owner driven cabs.

The uninhibited growth of the medallion in the early sixties pointed to some fundamental problems within the industry. The value of the medallions, both fleet and owner driven, had increased during the fifties and early sixties without an equitable distribution of the monopoly profits accrued. This was nowhere more true than in the case of the fleet medallion. During the forties, fifties and early sixties the major fleet owners of the city were free to dictate wage contracts and commission systems to suit their fancy. The taxi unions during this period were no more than pathetic examples of union racketeering and corruption. In fact, these unions were nothing more than paper locals which served to deter real unionizing attempts. Under these conditions the value of the fleet-owned medallion inevitably soared. The monopoly was near perfect and profits were barely shared with the fleet drivers.

All of this changed, however, with the creation of the Taxicab Drivers Union under Harry Van Arsdale. The first contract negotiated in the late spring of 1966 raised the commissions of all drivers to 46 percent and provided that the percentage would be further raised to 47 percent by December of 1966.[2] The price of the medallion fell off accordingly, dropping from a peak value of $35,000 to $22,000 by October of 1966. The owners no longer were able to indiscriminately exploit the value of the monopoly created for them by city ordinance. Furthermore, most of the large fleets suffered from a lack of manpower and were not making as much money as they thought possible. Part of the reason was due to the conspicuous lack of licensed cab drivers during the early sixties. A bare minimum of drivers were employed in the industry during the years 1960 to 1965. However, the lack of man power reflected the disinterest of most job seekers in working for a low paying profession at a time when the general economy was in good shape. With the increase in commissions under the union contract wages were increased but the industry was unable to enlist enough new drivers to keep all their cabs on the streets. This lack of manpower, which was aided by the police department's notorious lethargy in processing applicants, further contributed to the decline in the value of the medallion.[3] If the cab was not driven, it stood to reason the medallion would drop in value. The following graph depicts the rise and fall of the medallion empire ruled by the major New York fleets.

Since the creation of the Taxicab Union in 1966, the value of fleet medallions has been consistently declining. Nevertheless, the union was not the only reason for the fall of this monopoly which was valued at over a third of a billion dollars at its peak. The enormous value of the Taxi Industry's monopoly triggered an unprecedented growth in stealing and other dishonest or illegal rackets to cash in on the wealth enjoyed by the owners of the industry. Everybody near or involved in the industry saw the potential profit to be made. The two major catalysts in the continued fall of the taxi empire and the price of the medallion, after the creation of the Van Arsdale union, were the growth in off-the-meter negotiations and the growth in the gypsy cab industry.

The first problem was strictly a fleet owner's concern; however, the existence of the gypsy was an ill omen for the entire industry. It signalled the dissolution of the taxi empire, albeit at the hands of illegal or dishonest cab drivers and gypsy drivers. Even the value of the owner-driver medallion dropped in the early seventies, reflecting the emergence of an alternate competitive form of taxi service. The graph of the value of the owner-driver medallion clearly indicates that the medallion lost much of its value in the seventies as gypsy competition increased and the taxi industry's empire doubled in size.

Cost Inefficiency: The Hot Potato

The rapid rise in the value of the fleet owned medallions during the fifties and early sixties led to an increase in the volume of medallions sold on the black market. Many large companies folded in the early sixties or changed hands. Notable examples were the liquidation of the National Transportation Company (owning 965 cabs) in the early sixties and the transfer of the Terminal Transportation System into the hands of the Yonkers Raceway Corporation. These transactions along with a continuous stream of smaller sales have resulted in an average of 700 to 1,000 medallion sales per year.[5] Although the largest volume of sales has involved owner-driver medallions, the sale of fleet medallions has had the most profound consequences on the cost efficiency of the industry.

The transfer of the medallion cost from one operator to another has meant that new operators automatically have had economic disadvantages over those who have owned their medallions since 1937. The medallion cost as a result has become a large part of the overhead for the most recent individuals and companies entering the taxicab industry.

The additional overhead of the medallion has aggravated the financial well-being of the entire industry. It has become, along with the union

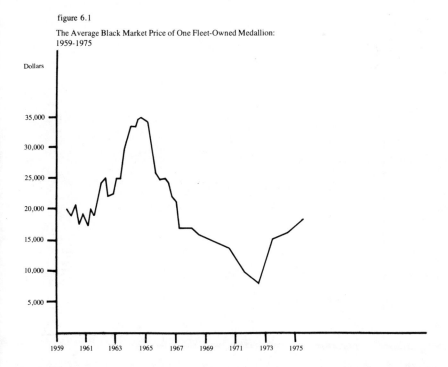

figure 6.1

The Average Black Market Price of One Fleet-Owned Medallion: 1959-1975

contract, gypsy cab competition and the driver's stealing, a poison to the life of the industry. The fleet owners' costs have escalated enormously during the decade of the sixties and have brought a long trail of bankruptcy proceedings in the wake of the growing operating costs. However, not all fleet owners are on the brink of disaster. Those who have been hurt the most are the companies which purchased their medallions during the peak years of the sixties and are located in areas of the city where gypsy competition has proved to be the strongest.

The financial ruin of the taxi industry has not been a private affair. The industry has consistently passed their operating costs onto the public. Instead of eliminating inefficient procedures of service, the fleet owners have banded together under the Metropolitan Taxi Board of Trade and have legislated for fare increases that have allowed inefficient operators to stay in business. For the first time in 50 years the price of a taxi ride, relative to the consumer price index, began climbing in the sixties and early seventies. However over the last few years the increasing cost of cab service has been offset by an even faster increase in the cost of living. The net effect has been that cab service has dropped in cost without an increase in ridership. This is clearly seen in the graph.[6]

Taxi service in New York historically had been one of the best bargains in town. Since the beginning of the taxi industry in 1907, there had been

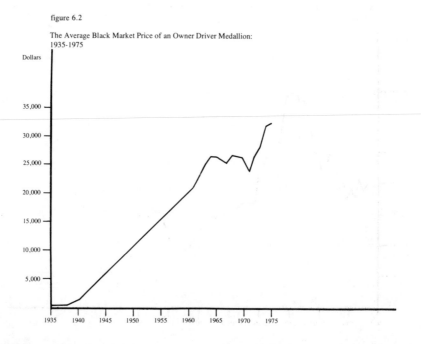

figure 6.2

The Average Black Market Price of an Owner Driver Medallion:
1935-1975

a consistent decline in the cost of an average taxi ride when adjusted to the consumer price index. The relative low cost of taxi service in New York had been possible because of the large volume of business and the high operating efficiency of taxicabs. In New York, unlike any other American city, the density of traffic had allowed the rates to remain low.

With the passage of the Haas Act in 1937, low cost taxi service was soon eliminated. There have been five fare hikes since 1937 and all of them have raised the price of taxi service. In addition, four of the five fare hikes passed since 1937 have occurred in the last decade. In comparable periods of time before and after the Haas Act of 1937, significant differences can be seen. Prior to 1937 every fare rate structure passed by the city council reduced the price of taxi service, whereas just the opposite has occurred since then. Between 1900 and 1937 the cost of an average taxi ride dropped 40 percent, whereas in the 38 years following the Haas Act, the cost of unadjusted taxi service has increased 250 percent.

The rise in the price of taxi service reflects the growth of inefficient producers of service. The medallion has been the key to the whole problem. It has been transfered from one owner to another like a hot potato. Those who have held onto the hot potato too long have gone bankrupt; those who have passed it along, have eventually passed it to the public. Nobody wanted to get stuck with the cost of paying off an overpriced medallion. However, those who did, and didn't have the sense to sell it and recoup some of their

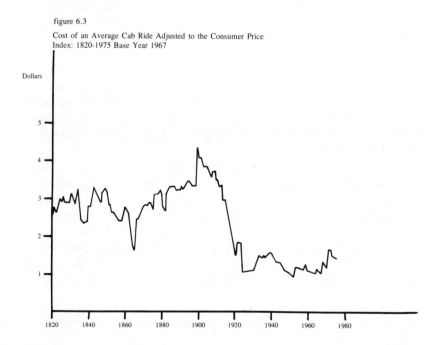

figure 6.3

Cost of an Average Cab Ride Adjusted to the Consumer Price Index: 1820-1975 Base Year 1967

losses, have attempted to turn their loss into profit at the public's expense.

Public Policy and Private Interests:
City Hall Protects the Owners

The city council has been largely responsible for the fact that the public has paid for the rising cost of medallions through rising service costs. No standards of operating efficiency nor public investigations of the cost structure of the industry have ever been made by the members of the city council. They have simply relied on the data and the public accountants hired by the fleet owners as their guide to establishing an equitable fare rate structure. Inevitably, this has meant that one city administration after another has acceded to the cost structure of the fleet owners. The most inefficient operators have passed their burden onto the entire industry, represented by the Metropolitan Taxi Board of Trade, and the industry has passed it to the city council which in turn has passed the responsibility for the whole mess to the taxi riding public.

As a group, the fleet owners have been a very powerful lobby. Represented by the Metropolitan Taxi Board of Trade, the fleet owners have held a virtual stranglehold over the city council. In part, the growing political strength of the MTBOT reflects the consolidation of economic and political power in the hands of a few. In 1937 there were 380 separate fleet companies operating in New York. By 1966 the number had shrunk to 86 then to 65 in 1972 and by 1975 there were no more than 52 large fleets. Although the number of companies has drastically shrunk in 35 years, the total number of fleet taxis has remained unchanged. Presently, the medallioned taxi industry is limited to 11,787 taxis of which 6,816 are fleet-owned and 4,971 are owned and operated singly. Despite the relatively large numbers of fleet-owned taxis, a growing consolidation of power has taken place. Although only 58 percent of all taxis are fleet-owned, 70 percent of those taxis are in fleets of 100 or more and 18 percent are in fleets of 300 or more.[8] This is in striking contrast to the diversity of fleet sizes in the 1930s when no more than 26 percent of all taxis were operated in fleets of 100 or more.

Presently, 24 families comprising 60 individuals have controlling shares in 27 companies operating 42 percent of all the city's taxis.[9] An additional 12 percent of the fleet taxis are under the ownership of the Terminal Transportation System and the Eden Transportation System, representing the third and the largest fleets respectively. The Terminal Transportation System owned by Yonkers Raceway since 1961 and Eden Transportation System established by the Eden family and associates in the sixties are the only exceptions to the tight knit family rule of the industry. This family web which has spread over the industry in the last twenty years has facilitated the process of making industry-wide decisions. Furthermore, the industry has consolidated its public image under the banner of the MTBOT which has served as the principal bargaining agent for all but two of the city's fleets.

During bargaining sessions with the city council, the MTBOT has exerted a strong grip over the political decisions made. Owner-drivers, whose economic structure varies widely from that of the fleet owners, have been perfectly content to allow the larger fleet operators to dictate the price structure for the industry as a whole. From their standpoint, their operating costs have not merited fare hikes; however, they have been perfectly content to institute higher fares as long as the medallion empire remains intact. The city council, suffering from political apathy, has not established guidelines to promote the efficient operators and weed out the inefficient ones. Instead, it has allowed the weakest businesses to dictate the policies for all businesses, with no consideration being given to the varying cost structures of the industry.

The approach of the present city council to the problems of the taxicab industry is a far cry from the approach taken at the turn of the century. In the case of the Yellow Taxicab Company vs. William J. Gaynor, the court gave the following decision:

> No one is bound to provide or operate any particular kind of a vehicle or motor vehicle, and if the rate of fare fixed by the board of aldermen is not sufficient to allow motor vehicles to be operated in the streets of the city of New York profitably to the owners, then the owners can cease from such operations.[10]

This decision clearly pointed to the public nature of taxi service. The taxi industry is still vested with a public interest; however, today, public policy has fallen prey to private interests. Private backroom decisions involving the captains of industry have set the standards for taxi service as it exists today.

The Owners Cut Costs:
The Drivers and the Public Bear the Burden

The industry has not limited itself to manipulating the political structures of the city, since political deals alone have not been able to salvage its sinking economy. As a result, the industry has taken some very desperate moves to stay its economic deterioration. The industry's costs, above and beyond the expenditure of owners still paying off loans on medallions, have been the cost of the automobiles, rising gasoline prices, the union contract and the phenomenal growth in off-the-meter negotiations.

Since the spring of 1969 the industry has systematically taken steps to reduce the cost of automobiles, reduce the union contract and eliminate all the taxi bandits.[11]

The owners' first broad program for reducing costs and increasing their profits was to install a device known as a "hot seat" in all taxis. This program started in December of 1968 and as of the summer of 1972 nearly all of the city's fleets had installed these passenger detection systems. The fleet owner's response to the pervasive practice of cheating among the hack profession has met with some success. However, the hack has responded in turn with his own set of tools. New technology has created new driver skills and these skills have undermined the owner's program of increasing his profits.

In a sense, the owners have been content to allow the practice of cheating to continue, because they realize that this particular aspect of the profession remains one of the few enticements to the driver. With low wages, gypsy cab competition, and hundreds of other frustrations plaguing the cabby, cheating becomes one of his few pleasures. Although the owners would like to cash in on the stolen money, they sense that an extreme reform of the drivers' ethics could eliminate their labor force or entice them to become gypsy drivers. Since the installation of the hot seats, there has been a noticeable emigration of drivers to companies that have been without the device; an omen that caused many owners to relax their use of the hot seat.

Because of the difficulty of thwarting the practices of dishonest cab drivers, the industry has turned to alternate schemes in order to postpone its death. Safety and the cost of repair of an automobile are intimately related. If it proves to be possible to run a cab into the ground at no extra cost, the fleet owners will forego the worries of possible mechanical defects and inadequate inspections of the cab and attempt to milk their cabs for their full worth. The cab is an expense as well as an important depreciation item in their operating expenses. In so many words, the fleet owner has taken the position, "let's push it as far as it will go and then junk it." In this way he manages to decrease the fringe costs of his operation and prolong the use of his cabs.

In the last four years an increasing number of fleets have prolonged their replacement cycle from the standard 12 to 18 month period to as long as three years. If a fleet of taxis can be operated for that many years without replacement, the owner is able to cut his overhead and turn a larger profit on his investments.

The owner's present policy of extending the life of each cab has had dangerous consequences. Minimal repairs and thread bare comforts have made a taxi ride unsafe at any speed. Not only is the passenger uncertain of the mechanical safety of the vehicle, but the driver is never sure from moment to moment how long his cab will keep running.

The unwillingness of the fleet owners to keep their vehicles well tuned or to replace their fleets when they are beyond repair has directly threatened the quality of the urban atmosphere. Approximately one half of all New York's taxicabs failed to pass the emission standards set for taxicabs in 1972.[12] The effect is that half of all mobile-source air pollution in midtown Manhattan is directly attributable to the taxi industry.[13] Although the taxi industry's public relations men, better known as hack P.R. men, deny any wrongdoing, the fleet owner's desire to cut down on expenses has directly threatened the lives of the general public.

In the light of these policies, the Taxi and Limousine Commission attempted to bar the operation of mechanically unsound vehicles. This brought the fleet owners to their final ploy—the destruction of union strength and a reduction of their labor costs. As their effort to turn the tide of bankruptcy, the owners have markedly reduced the commission for all new drivers. This has been the most effective stopgap measure instituted so far. Lower wages and an increased effort to hire new drivers has torn asunder the first genuine taxi union in the history of the City of New York. Although the owners have prevailed over the union, they have done so at the expense of alienating labor from the hack profession.

Further Efforts to Cut Costs:
Return to System of Production Quotas

The fleet owners have used the lowered commission rate as an alternative means of establishing production quotas within the industry. In light of the fact that the hot seat has failed to eliminate the practice of cheating among drivers, the owners have used the lowered commission rate as a means for compensating for the enormous sum stolen by the driver. However, its presence within the industry has had profound psychological effects. The owners have created panic among the older drivers since they are of the opinion that the lowered commission is a device to make them work harder for fear of being replaced by a younger driver, or even worse, to phase them out entirely.

Presently fleet owners expect each driver to bring in approximately 42 dollars per shift to be considered sound labor investments. If the driver consistently "books" less than the average production quota for the entire fleet, the owner will call him in to discuss the situation or flatly fire him for being a low booker. Because of these thinly veiled threats to the driver's occupation, the production quota has forced all drivers concerned with job security to compete with each other to maintain their jobs.

The intent of Van Arsdale's union was to eliminate this practice and offer all members a guaranteed job regardless of their ability to produce service to the public. This, however, has not been achieved. Many drivers are blacklisted by the fleet owners' trade association, making it impossible for them to switch garages and start again. As long as the fleet owner can maintain a large supply of available labor to replace all drivers he finds to be unacceptable, he has no obligation to individual drivers, nor any real fear of the union taking reprisal.

There has been very little that the union has been able to do to limit the owners' indiscriminate ability to fire drivers. Throughout the history of the industry, the many taxicab unions that have organized the hack profession have been unwilling and unable to establish secure jobs for all their members. This has been due to the union's inability to limit its total membership. As a result the present union as well as all of its predecessors has been unable to guarantee a job to the man who pays his dues and has been denied the right to drive a cab. Occasionally strikes have been called by drivers to protest the firing of a low booker. However, over the past 65 years none of these timid strike gestures ever succeeded in eliminating the production quota system.

Due to the union's inability to provide job security, alternate measures have long existed to protect the driver's job. When all else fails and the driver finds himself without a job, or the support of the union, graft opens the door, In fact, this situation is the rule of the profession. To be assured of getting a cab many drivers will kick back a certain amount of money to the dispatcher. This, then, has been the sad history of job protection in the New York taxi industry. As the Taxicab Survey of 1934 stated:

> The system works toward the oppression on the part of the irresponsible employer or his dispatcher. With the competition for jobs, not only can the dispatcher demand graft, but the owner can demand that the driver report and turn in a minimum amount of his bookings whether or not he really registered that amount.[14]

In effect, job protection is a product of the conniving relationship of the dispatcher and owner with the helpless hack. Even drivers who are good bookers and dependable workers will customarily "tip" the dispatcher to stay within his good graces. In this way they can be certain that they will receive prompt attention when they want to take out a cab and have a good chance of getting a cab that is in good condition.

With the introduction of the reduced commission rate for new drivers, the production quota has become a tool for the potential elimination of entire segments of the taxi labor force. Many older full-time drivers working under the 50 percent commission rate are fearful that the production quota will be used as an excuse to eliminate them so as to install a labor force working the reduced commission rate. Whether or not this fear has been realized is not the crucial issue. The real issue is the existence of a graded commission system. Originally the lower commission rate was instituted to professionalize the industry by creating a three year apprenticeship program under which drivers would gradually achieve the same wage contract of seasoned drivers. In return, the union was to be granted the right to set up a central hiring hall for the entire industry. In effect Van Arsdale allowed the owners to institute an unfavorable commission system in the hope that the union could create a closed shop within the industry. Van Arsdale had pinned his hopes on a pipe dream. A closed shop agreement has not been established, nor is it likely that it ever will be. However on the hope of meeting this end Van Arsdale traded away ten years of union achievements.

The implications of the present labor agreements have been that the owners have increased their part-time labor force at the lower commission rate and have been slowly phasing out the older drivers ready to retire. In truth the owner's ploy was not aimed at professionalizing the ranks of the hack driver, it was a sophisticated technique for maintaining what has always been a part-time industry, at an ever lower commission rate. These factors, first an increase in the number of new drivers coupled with the fact that 50 percent of all drivers are part-timers (therefore not eligible for bonus pay) and second, the fact that over 50 percent of all cab drivers retire within three years of acquiring a license, suggest that the fleet owners are seriously threatening the existence of the union, not to mention the profession.

The political effects of the "sellout contract" have been tremendous. The membership of the union felt betrayed by its leaders and fearful for its jobs in the wake of the fleet owners' recruitment, designed to increase the number of new drivers. In reaction to its contract conspired between the union and the fleet owner, the drivers united without regard to status. The full-timers have demanded the elimination of the graded commission system for fear of their jobs and the part-timers have used the occasion to demand proportional rights. In addition, all the new drivers working full time under the reduced commission rate have joined the ranks of the dissatisfied. The result of the alliance of the disinherited and dissatisfied has been the creation of an organization called the Rank and File Coalition. The job security desired by older drivers near retirement found common ground with the part-timer's wishes for a share of the union benefits. The new coalition became the first threat to the historical allegiance of the older drivers with their union leadership. The shift in allegiance of older drivers to an opposing Van Arsdale faction represented the first indication of the division of the union. Where the union once stood uncontested and strong, a growing number of drivers became dissatisfied with the possible consequences of Van Arsdale's long range maneuvers to strengthen his union. In essence, Van Arsdale's efforts to bargain for a stronger union in the distant future were threatened by the immediate fears of his constituency, who dissolved the uncontested strength of his organization and allowed the fleet owners greater control over all collective bargaining.

Although the owners have managed to lower commissions, hinder the practices of blatant cheaters and ignore the mechanical condition of their vehicles, they have been unable to eliminate the continued growth of the gypsy cab. The owners have attempted to legislate them out of existence by demanding that municipal government enforce the law; however, the existence of these illegal operations points to some fundamental problems in the nature of taxi service that defy the enforcement powers of the police.

Economics Of The Driver

Deterioration Of Public Service

The presence of the gypsy cab on the streets of New York is just another example of the failure of the taxi industry to properly serve the public. The owner's desire to protect his assets from public liability incurred through accidents, his unwillingness to maintain his vehicles in sound mechanical condition as well as his ability to force the public to pay for his cost inefficiency through repeated fare hikes are indications of the failure of the taxi industry to operate for the vested interests of the public.

The driver in turn, since he is influenced by the organization and limitations under which the industry operates, has extended the problems of taxi service. The powerful monopoly established by the Haas Act in 1937 eventually created a demand for taxis far outstripping their availability. Since 1937 the taxi industry has exploited the most lucrative taxi market in the world. New York's central business district became more prosperous, reflected in the vertical growth of the city, which in turn allowed the cab driver to restrict his service to the smallest and most lucrative area of the city. The effect of this development has been consistent refusal to serve the residents of New York's ghettoes.

Hacks consider the New York ghettoes to be the Achilles heel of the occupation. Ghettoes such as Harlem, Bedford Stuyvesant, Brownsville, East New York, Jamaica, South Bronx, the Lower East Side, and Morrisania, to mention but a few, have been consistently snubbed by the New York hack. The problem of inadequate ghetto service became a major issue in the decade of the sixties with the rise in the number of poor blacks and Puerto Ricans entering the city. The all too visible lack of service provided by the medallioned taxi aggravated the hostility and frustration ghetto residents have felt toward the public services of the city.

The driver is not all to blame for the service problem in the ghettoes. His actions reflect some of the larger problems of the industry and the city as a whole. Historically the major causes of service refusal have been the risk of robbery, racial discrimination against ghetto residents, the economic factor of discrimination (favoring the central business district) and the competitive warfare with the gypsy cab. These problems have come to a head in the last few years with the explosion of taxi robberies, dramatic increases in the number of gypsies and a 100 percent increase in the price of a taxi ride. The situation has been getting worse and it appears there is no solution that will improve taxi service in the ghettoes. In effect the ghettoes have now become the domain of the gypsy cab.

Crime

Since 1959 New York's ghettoes have steadily earned the reputation for being hotbeds for crime. In particular, drivers have been the victims of an increasing number of stick-ups in those areas with the heaviest concentration of blacks and Puerto Ricans. This problem has reached epidemic proportions in the last four years. From 1968 to 1970 there was an average annual increase of 95 percent in the number of taxi robberies reported to the police.[1] The 60 percent rise in general robberies throughout the city between 1969 and 1971 was far less dramatic than the 120 percent rise in taxi robberies during the same period.[2] The following list gives the annual volume of reported taxi robberies:

1963 — 438	1968 — 920	1973 — 1,908
1964 — 507	1969 — 1,283	1974 — 1,864
1965 — 644	1970 — 3,208	
1966 — 940	1971 — 2,360	
1967 — 720	1972 — 1,553	

The driver is perhaps the most vulnerable target of crime in the city. The rules governing hacks require the cab driver to serve any and all people desiring his services. This inevitably has placed the driver in a precarious situation since he can not legally refuse a suspicious fare, nor does he wish to be the unwitting victim of robbery. For most drivers the solution has been to stay away from those areas where robbery is most likely to occur or to refuse to take passengers anywhere near the crime zones.

Regardless of the driver's determination, it is virtually impossible for him to avoid crossing or entering high crime areas of the city, since the taxi robber is not limited to any specific area of the city in which to commit the robbery. In this situation the city as a whole becomes a jungle of crime. Drivers are well aware of their constant vulnerability and this has made them doubly fearful of entering areas of the city with a reputation for crime.

Although the largest number of taxi robberies take place in areas with predominantly black and Puerto Rican populations, these areas do not entice any taxi business. Nearly 80 percent of all the robberies in Manhattan are in Harlem or the Lower East Side.[4] In fact, Harlem's 28th and 32nd precincts alone accounted for 40 percent of all the robberies in Manhattan in 1971. It is therefore not without reason that cab drivers hesitate to enter the ghetto. They realize that very few cabs travel through black areas, yet a high percentage of all the robberies commited throughout the city happen in these very same places.

A conservative estimate of 70 percent of all the taxi robberies occur in black or Puerto Rican ghettoes. This is an extremely high percentage in light of the fact that over 60 percent of all taxis operate in Manhattan.[5] In effect, it means that every taxi entering an outer borough ghetto is like a duck in a shooting gallery. The driver has little recourse but to turn the money over to the thief and pray that his life be spared.

The vast majority of taxi robberies are perpetrated by the passenger

rather than a person directly off the street. This situation tends to complicate the already chaotic and impersonal relationship between the driver and passenger. In fact it has made many drivers blind with fear. A sad but amusing example of this was related by a taxicab robber who held up a driver with a coke bottle. The bandit placed the spout to the driver's neck and demanded his money. The driver, frozen with fear, was duped into believing the gun was for real. This is by no means an unusual example of the techniques used by desperate addicts in need of a quick fix. The New York Police Department reports that well over 50 percent of all taxi holdups are perpetrated by individuals using guns or simulated guns while knives and physical force are used in one third and one tenth of all holdups respectively. Often as not, the bandit will use a knife or toy gun since the cost of buying a real gun is often beyond his budget.

Economics of Discrimination

The fear of crime and robbery supports a further problem of ghetto service. Drivers are reluctant to serve blacks and Puerto Ricans destined for ghetto areas, due to the economic consequences of deadheading back from these areas. No driver wants to waste time by going out of an area where fares are to be found: that just means he has to double back to the nearest cruising route and in the interim he has wasted a good deal of valuable time. In theory the driver wants to maximize the number of passengers he can carry in a ten hour day since more money can be made in a shorter time off the initial drop of the meter than by taking long trips. New York's black ghettoes bear the brunt of the cabby's economic discrimination due to their geographical distance from the heart of the city. Ghettoes such as Bedford Stuyvesant, Brownsville, East New York, Jamaica, the South Bronx, and Morrisania have not been served well because these areas are economically less rewarding than the central business district of Manhattan. Economic discrimination is a very powerful component of the quality and quantity of service offered by the medallioned industry. It is not simply a problem confronted by ghetto residents but by all New Yorkers living in the suburban outer boroughs.

Nevertheless the problem of obtaining taxi service is worse for a black or Puerto Rican, since their image is compounded by the problem of ghetto crime. Whether the driver wants to or not, he must soon realize that black and Puerto Ricans are his biggest threat. Under these conditions it is often very hard for a driver to abandon his stereotype of the taxi robber and accept blacks as he does whites. In this fashion ghetto crime and the economic inequalities of long haul service reinforce the problem of racial discrimination.

One older driver related his racial fears in this way:

> Of course generally speaking, let's face it, you avoid picking up blacks. Now I picked up quite a few recently and there's an amazing thing you have to remember that all blacks don't live in Harlem or Bedford Stuyvesant. Especially lately more and more are living in midtown [Manhattan]. So I've been fairly lucky in who I've picked up. Now of course if he looks if he's past thirty I won't hesitate but if he's young and big and he's a kid of eighteen or nineteen. No way, no way. I'm not taking him. Because never mind this business of not getting held up, chances are you won't get paid. And that can happen with white kids too. If they're seventeen or eighteen or nineteen years old I don't want 'em, cause they'll run out on you and who needs the aggravation.

Oftentimes blacks will get the benefit of the doubt if they are well dressed and are stepping out of a respectable building. But this is no guarantee. As far as the cabby is concerned, it's not just the clothes that make the man but his final destination as well. If the hack has to go to Harlem, he knows he won't pick up a return fare because he is not interested in taking any chances: this attitude denies a ride to even the best dressed black man.

Since 1967 the price of an average taxi ride has risen from $1 to $1.35 in 1968 and finally to $2.25 in 1975.[6] Furthermore, the initial cost of hiring a cab has risen from 35 cents in 1967 to 45 cents in 1968 and then to the rate of 65 cents in 1975. This is in effect more than a doubling of the cost of riding by taxi and a 86 percent increase in the initial cost of hiring a taxi. Taxi drivers can now afford to be choosy and in fact are more likely to take short hauls to maximize the number of initial drops (initial cost of hiring a taxi) than they are to make a long haul. It stands to reason that the economic advantages of short trips work to the disadvantage of ghetto residents and residents of the outer boroughs.

Coupled with this, the increase in the cost of taxi service has also made it difficult for many people to afford its services. The poor people of the city find the cost of a taxi ride prohibitive and are provided with no substitutes. The taxi industry has implicitly denied its services to the poor by raising its price to luxury status. Surely this was not a decision vested with public interest!! In effect, the poor are excluded from the use of a necessary service and offered no alternative. The mass transportation system of the city can not substitute for the services of the taxi in providing short hauls within the ghetto neighborhood.

The economics of discrimination have made it less likely that a ghetto resident will travel by cab and have made the driver less willing to provide that service. In effect, this prevents taxi service from adequately serving the ghetto.

Racial Discrimination

The allegations of racial discrimination meted out by the Commission on Human Rights in 1966 failed to perceive the subtleties of the problem.[7] Although it is true, on the face of it, that racial discrimination exists within the ranks of the hack profession, it is somewhat deceptive to blame the problem on that alone. The hack profession has more than its share of bigots, yet these men are not the source of the major problem. As long as the cab driver is left defenseless and unprotected, his only defense left is discrimination; and unfortunately the correlation between taxi robberies and blacks is not conjectural. Out of the 1,212 reported taxi robberies during the first nine months of 1972, 72 percent were committed by blacks. In fact, during several months of 1972 the number of robberies perpetrated by blacks reached as high as 90 percent of all the reported robberies.[8] This puts the driver in the unfortunate situation of gauging the threat of crime by the color of one's skin. Undoubtedly, racial discrimination exists, but in the context of the taxi industry it is almost a necessary system of defense, albeit crude.

Competitive Warfare and Safety Systems

Beyond the liabilities of robbery and the economic and racial inequities of ghetto taxi service, the New York hack has been faced with a growing number of legal and illegal competitors from within the black community. These neighborhood oriented car services have sprung up over the last 12 years to meet the demands for transportation within the ghettoes of New York. The advent of the gypsy cab and private livery vehicle has caused severe problems for the medallioned taxi industry. As will be discussed in the following chapter, the medallion taxi is no longer able to claim sole dominion over the entire city as it was able to do for its first 50 years in New York.

The gypsy cab has not only begun to serve outer borough residents more adequately than the medallioned cab, it has deterred taxi drivers from serving the black community. Cab drivers are often intimidated and driven off the road through a show of force from the private livery or gypsy cab operators. It is not at all uncommon for a gypsy cab driver to cut off a medallion taxi from a prospective passenger and snatch that passenger up himself.

These black operated car services insist that their presence on the streets is merely a reflection of the persistent lack of service provided by the medallioned taxi. Indeed this is quite true although the existence of these neighborhood car services has accelerated the departure of the medallioned taxi from the black communities of the city. The private liveries and gypsy operators are not serving as a temporary substitute service for the taxi while the problems of the industry and the ghetto are ironed out: quite the contrary, their presence is a first step toward the eventual hope of monopolizing ghetto taxi service and achieving the status of the medallion taxi. These designs have jolted the poise of the medallioned fleet owners and forced them to develop counter measures and threats to their adversaries.

Since 1969 fleet owners of medallioned taxis have attempted to regain the favor of ghetto residents. They have urged the black community to, "ride yellow, ride safe" in an effort to smear the image of the black operated private liveries and gypsies. In actuality the fleet owners never entertained the notion that they might be able to regain the allegiance of the black community: all they were concerned with was limiting the expansion of the private livery and gypsy vehicles into areas still controlled by the medallion taxi industry. Unfortunately their efforts have met with little success. Not only are their adversaries stronger and more united than ever in the black communities, they have also threatened to infiltrate white middle class neighborhoods throughout the city.

Fleet drivers have been unable to compete effectively with the private livery and gypsy cab operations. This is in part due to the fact that taxi robberies have increased as dramatically as the number of gypsy and public livery competitors. Fleet drivers have insisted on some form of self-protection as a necessary prerequisite for better ghetto taxi service, stating that, "Although it may be safe for the taxi robber to ride yellow, I'd like to know about my own security."

The installation of bullet resistant partitions between the driver and the passenger has been a recent development, in fleet-owned cabs. In fact, it was not until the fall of 1971 that all fleet-owned taxis were outfitted with partitions. This still left 95 percent of all owner-driven taxis unprotected.[9] This group of individuals has been of the opinion that the black community is a lost market, feeling no efforts ought to be wasted on improving rapport at this late stage. The fleet driver, on the other hand, is now equipped to do battle with his rivals and fend off his assassins; yet he has lost faith in his cause and in his safety. Many drivers, in fact, regard the partition as a useless item with virtually no deterrent value at all. As one driver stated:

If a man wants to stick you up, he can come out to pay you at your window and then put a knife or gun to your throat and get you there. So the partitions are really not that great. No air circulates through the cab at all. It's just another gimmick to sell to fleet owners to annoy the driver.[10]

Furthermore, the cash boxes installed in all New York fleet taxis as of March 1971 have met with little driver approval. Nothing in the hack's opinion is totally effective against the determined stick-up man. Another driver claimed:

> If a robbery or other felony is to be committed, there is no real deterrent. If someone wants to commit a crime, they can and will, bullet resistant partitions, cash box notwithstanding.[11]

The driver's opinions are corroborated by the police department which reports that three out of every four taxis robbed in the first nine months of 1972 were equipped with a bullet resistant partition.[12] Although the partition has tended to reduce the possibility of murder, it has had absolutely no effect upon the determined taxi robber.

In fact one cab driver claimed that his partition was no more than a play thing on one occasion when he got robbed. He said'

> I took the wrong guy to the wrong place. I didn't have my wits about me. I was tired. I was going home one night and it was very cold. I was on third avenue in the fifties. Two couples were there with hardly any clothes on, for the winter anyway, and they begged me to take them to the Americana. So I said alright. So I was writing on the trip sheet after they got out and the next thing I hear a voice behind me, "135th and Madison." So I look. I couldn't even see the bastard in the mirror. I looked and he was hiding in the corner. I said "Where the hell did you come from?" He was dressed like he just got out of Yale five minutes before and he spoke with perfect diction. I says, "I ain't going to 135th and Madison. Even in the afternoon I don't." So we're arguing about it. "Don't worry I'll take care of you." Alright against my better judgement I took him. Well this was the old partition that were very loose. So when we got under the street light between 135th and Park and Madison, out of the corner of my eye I see this silver thing coming at me. So we battled for a while. See, he was through the partition now and he had a knife in his hand and I wasn't about to let go. He had something on his finger like a hook that these guys with newspapers use to pick up the bundles and he was trying to catch me in the throat and I didn't realize it until it started to hit me. We were eyeball to eyeball like this [he puts his face up to mine]. And I said "Do you wan't the money?" I don't even know what the hell I said. I said, "Get away from me, drop the knife on the floor and get in the back seat and I'll give you the cigar box," because there was all spooks around this whole block. And I had my windows up and I'm yelling "Rape, murder, everything." But nobody could hear me because all the windows were closed. I realized this later. So he gets in the back. I gives him the cigar box. We were in between two parked cars. So as he gets out he takes the partition with him because he was pretty burly.

VIDICH: He pulls it with him?

MEL: Yea. It was stuck on his shoulder.

VIDICH: The partition?

MEL: Yea the partition. That's how good they are. It's only held in by two little dinky screws. About this big [indicates a quarter inch long]. He was stuck in the partition and he got out the door while he tried to wiggle this thing [partition] out the door. I took off while he was half out the door and I let the door hit the bumper of a parked car. I thought maybe I killed him. You know. So I ran down Madison avenue, I was so excited. You know Madison avenue is one way. A cop grabs me about a few minutes after that. I was so excited. He says, "You're in the wrong precinct." I said "What the hell do you mean? I'm in the wrong precinct. Suppose I got stabbed what would you do? Let me lay there in the street?" "Don't get fresh," he said. So I had to go to another precinct. So I go there and I give the guy every wrong phone number. My own home wrong, the company's wrong. It took them a week to find me. The detective says, "I was beginning to think there was no hold up. You gave us every wrong phone number." They never found the guy anyway.

The ineffectiveness of all safety measures has helped to rigidify the boundaries of medallion service and create the climate for the growth and spreading of an enormous rival form of transportation. The partition and cash box have done little for the driver and far less for the passenger. Indeed, the very presence of protective armor on medallion taxis has irritated the black community. It is as if to say, "Your attitude toward our community has not changed at all except now you don't have to be as fearful of refusing to serve us."

The issue of inadequate ghetto service is exacerbated by the presence of many large fleet garages in the vicinity or in the midst of New York ghettoes. More than 60 percent of all taxi fleet garages in New York are in the vicinity or in the midst of a ghetto. Many of these fleets have been located in these areas since the thirties and forties; however, some fleet owners have been attracted to these areas because of the large supply of unskilled labor and low property costs. Undoubtedly, the fleets in the outer borough and black ghettoes have lower property costs and taxes than Manhattan based fleets although they have the additional problem that their drivers must commute to Manhattan to avoid the gypsy competition.

Many of the drivers living near their fleet garage have attempted to serve their own community; however, most are lured by the profitable midtown Manhattan area where fares are plentiful and the threat of robbery is minimal. The effect is that nearby residents in the ghetto are continually snubbed by off-duty taxis returning to their garages, heading to their garages or heading to the better hunting grounds in Manhattan. The driver will turn on his off-duty sign and cruise to the area he considers to be the best spot to nab fares. This was well documented by the Taxi and Limousine Commission Study on Service Refusal. The study found that as many as 25 percent of all the available taxis in Brooklyn were off duty at any time of day.[13] Perhaps even more dramatic was the fact that the taxis in the outer boroughs of New York were five to ten times more likely to be off duty than those in Manhattan. This is a clear example of the intent to deny public service to the outer borough residents.

Growth Of The Gypsy

Solution To Discrimination

The emergence of the gypsy cab operating in the outer boroughs of New York is a direct result of the failure of the medallion industry to supply services. The driver's unwillingness to serve the ghetto coupled with an unprecedented growth in the size of New York's ghettoes allowed the gypsy cab to enter the field and exploit a large black demand for taxi service.

Taxicabs, Liveries, Gypsies:
Their Legal Distinctions

According to the law, only taxicabs licensed by the city of New York are allowed to pick up passengers directly off the street. This law has existed since the days of the old hansom cab in order to protect the public against the possible abuses of the hack. The cab driver has always been closely regulated due to the ease with which disreputable drivers are able to victimize the public. Municipal licensing and regulation of the industry reflect this concern with consumer rights.

Private liveries unlike taxicabs are not licensed by the city of New York. Legally they may engage as a vehicle for hire in the state of New York only if they are licensed as an omnibus. This classification allows them to engage in private business arranged through *telephone requests* for service or agreements made within the confines of the livery garage. The private status of the livery in theory is compatible with the public status of the taxicab since they are both serving different demands for service and serving the public in different ways. However, the supposedly strong *legal distinction* between the two industries has been blurred by the advent of the latest taxi competitor: the gypsy cab.

The gypsy cab has been responsible for the breakdown of the legal distinctions between the taxicab and the private livery. The operators of these vehicles are either licensed liveries who flaunt the law and pick up passengers off the street or they are without licences of any sort. For the most part gypsies and liveries are synonymous terms since, as will be seen in this chapter, the lure of stealing business off the street (which is legally the right of only medallion taxis) entices the livery operator to act like a taxicab.

The rise of the gypsy cab industry in effect points to the growing demand for taxi service in the outer boroughs of New York. Its existence, unlike that of the law abiding private livery points to the failure of the medallion industry to meet the taxi needs of the city. With the growth of the city's population and the increased commercial importance of Manhattan in the nation and the world, a demand for taxi service has developed far outstripping the limited number of cabs available to supply this service. In effect the medallion industry has failed to monopolize taxi service in New York because the demand for its services has surpassed its ability to supply those services. The gypsy cab, as a surrogate taxi, represents a return to the days of free competition and laissez-faire capitalism within the industry.

It is not widely known that the private livery, otherwise called a gypsy cab, is the direct descendant of the private taxi, providing service to exclusive hotels, restaurants, theaters, and railroad terminals at the turn of the century. At that time, the private livery was legally required to organize its business operation by prearrangement, whether that was by a telephone call, a letter, or an agreement in person. The medallioned and nonmedallioned vehicles presently serving the city were in effect born of the same parents. It was only later that they began to develop separate characters. The separation of the two industries became a reality in 1913 when the city council affirmed the public nature of taxi service and required all vehicles licensed by the city to install taximeters. Those operations refusing to install taximeters were prohibited from engaging in public business through cruising or by using the public hack stands of the city.

It was at this juncture in the history of the taxi industry that the private livery operations began to fade in importance. The legal redefinition of their status forced many of them to go out of business or to transform their operations into public taxi operations or in the last resort to redevelop their businesses in areas unserved by the taxicab. It was not until the passage of the Haas Act in 1937, limiting the number of taxis in the city, that the private livery again began to play a significant role in the transportation of the city. Many of the present private livery operations in the city date back to that time when these operations were services provided to white middle class communities on the fringes of the city. In a sense these private liveries existed as a legal supplement to the service rendered by the medallioned cabs since there was no overlap between the markets served by the taxicab and the private livery operators. As long as the two industries were clearly defined and administrative ordinances were enforced, the common carrier status of the taxicab was totally compatible with the private carrier status of the private livery operations.

Today the increasing importance of the private livery in ghetto areas has been a consequence of the following developments spanning the last twenty years; the lack of adequate taxi service in the outer borough and the ghettoes, the growth of concentrated black and Puerto Rican population centers scattered throughout the outer boroughs, inadequacy of the bus and subway system in meeting the travel needs of the black and Puerto Rican communities, the relative immunity with which private liveries were able to operate as taxicabs accepting hails off the street and the casual nature of police supervision within the private livery industry.

Growth of the Ghetto: A New Market

Starting in the early fifties an increasing number of blacks and Puerto Ricans immigrated to the city. An estimated 1.7 million blacks and Puerto Ricans, mostly poor, made their homes in the city between 1950 and 1970.[1] This sharply increased the population of blacks and Puerto Ricans and further expanded the already large ghettoes of the city. With the growth in population over the last 20 years came a corresponding growth in the density of population; this was nowhere more true than in the ghetto. An estimated 81.6 percent of the city's black population in 1971 lived in the 26 designated poverty areas.[2] Furthermore, the greatest growth in the black and Puerto Rican population during the decade of the sixties was in the officially designated poverty areas of the city. The segregation of blacks and Puerto Ricans was made more apparent by another trend happening simultaneously: the exodus of 1.9 million whites, mostly middle class, during the past 20 years.[3] The result has been a growing racial polarization of the city, further evidenced in the high degree of residential segregation between blacks and whites.

The growing racial polarization of New York has become more apparent since WWII. The enormous increases in the size and density of the urban ghettoes of New York has been accompanied by a growth in the gypsy and private livery industries. In fact the areas in which the gypsy and private livery operators have expanded their operations over the last 20 years correspond precisely with the expansion of the black ghettoes of the city.

In this context, the black nationalism or isolationism which has arisen out of the ghetto supports the private livery industry. When a choice exists for a ghetto resident between a medallioned cab and a black operated private livery cab, the latter offers the passenger a feeling of allegiance with his people. Furthermore, community support has rallied behind the private liveries and strengthened the feeling that the transportation issue is a confrontation of the black owned and operated private liveries versus the big money white fleet owners and their white lackey drivers.

The distinction between the two industries is apparent since nearly 95 percent of all private livery drivers are black or Puerto Rican, whereas no more than 35 percent of all taxi drivers are black or Puerto Rican.[4] In addition, the language barrier of the Puerto Rican immigrant has placed Puerto Rican drivers of private livery services in an important role in aiding their urban mobility. The similar racial and cultural backrounds of the driver and passenger tend to create the personal appeal of travelling, "with your own kind." Indeed it is not quite as trying or emotionally as difficult to adjust to the complex and anonymous life of New York if the immediate people and businesses that become a part of one's daily life embody one's concerns, cultural heritage and social problems. The neighborhood private liveries fit this description.

The Ghetto—Isolated from Public Transport

The isolation and relative immobility of the residents of the black community has made the taxi or its substitute, the private livery, a vital part of their daily life. The issue is not whether there is a lack of luxury personalized transportation in the ghetto; it is a question of whether the poor are adequately served by the existing bus and subway systems and the extent to which poor ghetto residents have their own means of transportation. As would be expected, the residents of the black and Puerto Rican ghettoes are less likely to own an automobile for the simple fact that the level of unemployment is strikingly high and their annual income markedly lower than the rest of the city. Harlem with as many as 52 percent of all its families earning less than $4,000 in 1960 and the Lower East Side with 50 percent earning less than $4,000, both have the lowest level of automobile ownership.[5] Fewer than 15 percent of the families in these two areas own an automobile. The situation in the outer borough ghettoes is not quite as severe as that in Harlem and the Lower East Side; nevertheless it remains appreciably worse than that found in middle class neighborhoods of the city.

Among the patrons of private livery services as many as 45 percent do not own an automobile and nearly the equivalent number are living on an annual income of less than $7,000.[6] These figures are in striking contrast to the profile of the taxicab user whose annual income exceeds $10,000.[7]

The relative immobility of the ghetto resident is reinforced by the mass transit of New York, which is totally outdated and inadequate for those who most need it. The fixed routes of the subway system all are directed toward providing the maximum amount of accessibility to the central business districts of Manhattan, in an era when the center of the city is declining in importance. The radial pattern of subway routes no longer adequately accommodates the varied locations of employment and residence of New Yorkers. With the decline in the relative importance of the central city, interborough and intraborough travel has become more extensive despite the fact that there are only two subway lines providing circumferential travel.

Oscar Ornati in his book *Transportation Needs for the Poor* emphasized the relative importance of nearby employment for residents of the city's ghettoes, as opposed to work in Manhattan's central business district. He found that as income levels decreased, the borough of residence became more important as the location of work. He states:

> We must conclude that even where the poverty areas are located within Manhattan or very close to it (as in the case of the Bronx) the relative attraction of Manhattan employment locations is less for low income workers than for residents of non-poverty neighborhoods.[8]

Thus workers living in poverty areas attempting to travel to job locations within their borough are often at an extreme disadvantage. Not only do most ghetto residents rely on mass transit more than middle income groups, they are also less likely to be adequately served by the established routes of mass transit. Even the bus system of the city offers little of an alternative to the subway since its adaptable nature has been nullified by the complexity and the lack of public information concerning its schedules and routes.

Furthermore, the blacks and Puerto Ricans, as the most recent immigrants to the city, tend to be the least familiar with the workings of the bus and subway system. Among patrons of private livery vehicles an estimated 15 percent are without immediate access to mass transportation in their neighborhood.[9] Furthermore, only two out of three private livery patrons actually have access to both bus and subway service within the confines of their neighborhood.[10] However, it should be kept in mind that the presence of mass transit within a neighborhood does not necessarily mean that the services provided by mass transit adequately coincide with the needs of the residents.

The obvious deficiencies of mass transit coupled with a glaring lack of public taxi service were instrumental in stimulating the growth of the private livery and gypsy cab industry.

Gypsies in Disguise: New Ways to Beat the System

Like many of the problems of the ghetto, the apparent illegality of the private livery operations was and continues to be overlooked by the police. Private livery operators, in order to remain legal, are required to obtain all of their business by prearrangement whether that be a telephone call or an off-the-street request for service. This legal system has broken down entirely; with very few exceptions those drivers legally licensed as private liveries have swollen the streets cruising for fares and operating as if they were taxicabs. As many as 75 percent of all private livery operators actually get all of their business from street hails.[11] This illegal practice is what first branded the industry as a band of gypsies, roving over the city without regard for the medallion taxi. In fact, today, the word "gypsy" is the slang expression most commonoly used to refer to the allegedly legal activities of the private liveries.

Virtually none of the private liveries have bothered to install two-way radios and very few actually get any part of their business through telephone requests. At most, only a quarter of all the liveries actually get any business at all from telephone requests and only a startling 15 percent can ascribe any portion of their business to the use of the two-way radio system.[12] In effect, these gypsy operators disguised as private liveries are working outside of the law. The relative lack of enforcement against gypsy activities has made their presence a direct threat to the entire medallioned taxi industry. By transforming a private livery into a full fledged gypsy operation, the driver is capitalizing on the monopoly value of the medallion taxi market without incurring the cost of buying the medallion. With the lack of police interest in enforcement, coupled with the growing value of the medallion and an increasing need for ghetto service, the decade of the sixties witnessed hoards of gypsies entering the market.

The enticement of operating one's own business has brought an enormous number of blacks and Puerto Ricans into the vehicle for hire trade, whether that be the legitimate liveries or the fly-by-night, illegal gypsy cabs.

To add insult to injury to the medallion fleet owners, the black operated car services have not only encroached upon medallion turf but have captured the allegiance of many of the disenchanted members of the medallioned industry. The problem has become so acute that fleet owners have

The shrewd and hardened face of this cab driver when looking for a fare often turns to rage when his competition steals his passengers right off the street. (Photograph by Paul Vidich)

stated that one out of every five gypsy or private livery drivers formerly drove a medallioned cab. In fact, a spokesman for the fleet owners states:

> There is an organized campaign to have gypsy drivers obtain hack licenses through regular channels. This is to serve the purpose of countering charges that they use only unqualified drivers. In the meantime, the number of new licenses—150 per week—are not joining our ranks, but are divided between both industries.[13]

To many of the medallion drivers, the gypsy cab operation represents the ultimate hustle of the fleet owner. In effect, these illegal operators are not merely siphoning off the profits from one single fleet owner but are cashing in on the value of the taxi industry's monopoly. Even for hacks having no aspirations to drive a gypsy cab, it is almost certain that the level of their hostility toward these illegal operators is the true measure of their admiration for gypsy operators. The growth of the gypsy industry above and beyond its threat to the concept of the medallion, has aggravated the long and intense discord between the hack and his boss. As a fleet spokesman states:

> Full time drivers work for the industry four days a week to maintain their benefits and are gypsies the balance of the week. Morale is undermined, and the frustration increases.[14]

In addition to the drivers' latent admiration for the gypsy operators is the fact that as many as 32 percent of all regularly employed fleet drivers have considered driving gypsy cabs.[15] Thus the hostility that many drivers hold for the gypsy operators expresses no more than a thinly veiled involvement in the possible economic advantages of these illegal operations.

Confusion on the Streets:
Return to Unregulated Competition

In theory a great deal of legal steps have been taken to cut the gypsy down to size or out of existence entirely. Nevertheless, those attempts have bordered more on scare tactics than on truly enforceable legislation.

The city ordinances during the decade of the sixties were concerned with maintaining the sharp and visible distinction between the city-licensed medallion taxis and all other vehicles. Rather than legally defining the status of the private livery and establishing regulations concerning its operation, the city ordinances passed during the sixties were concerned with limiting its encroachments into the medallion taxi market.[16]

Since 1955 the police department has systematically attempted to prohibit the use of any and all means of advertising which would deceive the public into believing that a private livery was a taxicab. Originally private liveries used to paint such words as "taxi" or "taxicab" or "hack" on the outside of the vehicle. This practice was prohibited by Local Law No. 82 in 1957.[17] Other techniques of masquerading as taxicabs, such as installing dome lights or roof lights similar to those used by taxicabs were prohibited by Local Law No. 68 the following year.[18] Nevertheless, a vast array of other techniques developed soon thereafter to replace the deception of the dome light and the written designation. A police department memorandum in the summer of 1963 chronicled the gypsies' skill at counter-subterfuge:

> One of the most prevalent means (of deception) is to paint their vehicles in colors and designs generally employed by licensed taxicabs. Another means is to paint a name on the door and trunk of their vehicles which incorporates the word "cap" or "car," and which is so printed as to be readily mistaten for "cab." In addition, outside lights other than roof lights are used so as to add to the misconception fostered by the color scheme and printing. Also rate schedules, simulating the rate schedules for licensed taxicabs, are posted on doors, to enhance the impression that the vehicle is a taxicab.[19]

Since 1963 the police department and its successor, the Taxi and Limousine Commission, have only eliminated one form of public deception, that being the imitation of the medallion taxi color schemes. As of 1970 all medallioned taxis were required to be painted yellow and private liveries were prohibited from using any color even suggestive of yellow. The remainder of the ploys used by the private liveries as outlined by the police memo remain as true today as ten years ago—in fact, more so.

In quite a comical fashion the gypsy and private livery drivers have taken to copying every change in stlye of the medallion cab. When the medallioned cabs were outfitted with decals stating, "licensed by the Police Department of N.Y." the gypsies soon followed with a similar decal stating, "Licensed by the state of New York under Charter No. " Gypsy drivers further mimic the medallion taxi by posting a fare rate sign similar to that employed by taxis, on the outside doors regardless of whether a meter is used to calibrate the cost of the ride.

Even today there are no laws prohibiting the use of taximeters in private livery vehicles. Ironically, the taximeter was one of the distinguishing trademarks of taxi service at the turn of the century when the taxi and the private livery were split into two different industries. The taximeter was felt to be the determining factor separating a public service from a private business operation. It is thus significant today that gypsy cabs and private liveries are using taximeters in their operations. The meter conveys the impression that a public service is being performed when in fact this is not the case.

Nobody has told these operators what to charge nor demanded the removal of their taximeters; all that has been required of this class of vehicles is that they conform to the omnibus licensing required of all New York State vehicles for hire.

In effect, the legal battles with the private liveries and gypsy operations have been interminable. For every law squelching the illegal activity or possible encroachment of private livery operations into the medallioned domain, there have arisen a dozen forms of new deception and subterfuge. The legal devices imposed by one city administration after another, limiting the operations of the private livery and gypsy cab have been taken in stride. Most drivers feel that every law has a loophole, which it is their responsibility to find or create if necessary. This attitude has allowed the illegal activity of the gypsy to proceed with little interference from the lawmakers down at city hall.

Like the hack driver, these illegal and legal ghetto car services share the same philosophical assumptions relative to their work; "You've got to cheat to make a living in this business." For the gypsy cab operators, the problem is not screening the passenger or worrying about the synchronized light system of New York; rather their concern is with cheating the medallion cab out of its business and evading police apprehension.

As much as he may wish to deny it, the owner or operator of a private livery is making his living off the street. There are precious few operators who are able to maintain a successful business by sticking to strictly legal prearranged business. Moreover, the lure and ease with which gypsy operators can steal business off the streets lessens their interest in pretending to work legitimately.

The gypsy driver rarely has problems when picking up a street hail. The difficulty comes afterward when the cop pulls out his court summons for illegal hacking. At this point the standard reply is, "But, sir, I can't help it if some guy hops into my car while I'm at a red light. What am I supposed to do, lock my doors?" "Listen, brother," the cop replies, "he ain't no friend of yours and this ain't no red light." Unlike the medallion cab driver, drivers of gypsy cabs are slow and stealthy. They slow down at every bar, catch every light and try to take the inside lane whenever there is a taxi nearby. Rarely will you find a driver of a gypsy cab racing lights and attempting to out hustle his opponents for the lead position on the street, as invariably occurs among taxi drivers. In fact, the slower they go the less a street hail looks like an illegal pick up and the more it looks like a prearranged affair.

"Hey man," says the gypsy driver, "I was just parked here minding my own business waiting for my man and you think I'm breaking the law." If the passenger is conversant with the standard gypsy ploys for beating the cops, he'll provide some further proof of the legitimacy of the operation. "Sir, I called him up a half hour ago, so he'd get here on time." What can a cop say to that? As long as the patrons of the gypsy cab operations are willing to conspire against the strict enforcement of the law, there is not much that can be done to halt their activities.

Police retaliation and counter measures of intimidating the gypsy drivers from making a living off the street have proved futile. In the summer of 1971 the newly organized Taxi and Limousine Commission attempted to institute mandatory fines of $200 for every private livery or gypsy found stealing business off the street.[20] The idea was a simple one; to make the possible costs of operating a gypsy far outweigh its benefits. This technique, however, has not been supported by the courts which have historically sided with the gypsy operations. The courts have been extremely lenient with the gypsies by reducing their fines to nominal fees and virtually condoning their activity in light of the woefully inadequate taxi service in the ghetto. In effect, the courts have worked to undermine the letter of the law in order to compensate for the inequalities caused by the existing legal monopoly of the medallioned industry. Rather than fully reprimanding the activities of the gypsy, the courts have been implicitly disagreeing with the law makers.

The Gypsy Becomes Legitimate

The growth of the gypsy cab and private livery industry has upgraded public recognition and provided a quasi-legal acceptance of their activities. With their growth in numbers, they have developed a sense of strength and with their virtual control over ghetto service, they have decreed a form of squatters' rights on taxi service. Although their business activities are virtually all in violation of the law, the private liveries have steadfastly defended their right to operate as taxicabs. Their major justification has been the hallowed myth of free enterprise, which they contend has been severely violated by the monopolistic medallion taxi industry. Nevertheless, most gypsy operators are not truly concerned with dissolving the medallion monopoly by legal edict nor are they interested in becoming fully regulated under the City Charter.

In effect, they do not want an open market any more than the medallion taxi industry, nor do they want to become part of the present medallion monopoly, for that would entail regulations, restrictions on their illegal activities and further licensing costs. All they really desire is an open market on cheating, since this is an orientation toward business that imposes few restrictions, and restrictions are what they are most adamantly attempting to destroy. An insurance spokesman for the private livery operations declared:

> We are not looking for power. We merely say that power is in the hands of those who are exploiting our communities, and that is intolerable. We are only seeking to capture the most limited objective of decency and to challenge the monopoly which has been feeding off us for 34 years.[21]

Their challenge to the medallion monopoly is a ruse; what the private livery operators are seeking is equal footing with the medallion cab without incurring the strains of unlimited competition. In truth, their philosophy of anti-monopoly has been used more as an emotional self-legitimatization for their presence on the streets than as an honest wish to transform the medallion taxi monopoly. Furthermore, the gypsy operators have no limited objectives when it comes to stealing from the medallion industry. Now that they have gained a semblance of control over their own neighborhoods within the city, they are beginning the larger task of conquering the medallion territory within the city. Their rhetoric has gone full circle; where it initially served as a self-defense for their existence, it has now turned into a reasonable justification for the continued expansion of their activities.

Decline Of The Medallion Industry

The proliferation of the gypsy cab industry was made possible by the benign negligence of the Lindsay administration. In the mid sixties Mayor Lindsay gave orders to stop ticketing the illegal gypsy cab operators in light of the glaring lack of taxi service in New York's ghettoes. This set a dangerous precedent within the field of public transportation, since it allowed unlicensed, unregulated operators to venture upon the streets with total immunity from legal mandates and police enforcement. Lindsay's motives for condoning the existence of the gypsy cab operators were a combination of political self-interest and a desire to rectify the inequities of taxi service created by the medallion concept. By favoring the gypsy operators, he was attempting to gain the political allegiance of the black and Puerto Rican community. Nevertheless, Lindsay saw the public significance of gypsy service in light of the woefully inadequate taxi service offered to the poor blacks and Puerto Ricans of the city. However, by personally sanctioning

the existence of these illegal operations, Lindsay and his administration
were remedying the problems of urban taxi service outside of the scope of
law and government. In the mid sixties a working relationship was established between the police department, the Lindsay political system and
those gypsies operating beyond the sanctions of the law. Under this convivi-
al partnership, the gypsy operators were without legal restraints since the
legal system was held in abeyance and the police department was ordered
to "keep hands off." The blanket protection offered by the Lindsay administration in 1966 allowed the number of gypsy cabs to double in six years.
Today there are more gypsies on the streets of New York than there are
medallion taxis; an estimated 15,000 to 19,000 gypsies ply the streets of New
York as compared to only 11,787 licensed taxis. Combined, the two industries have as many as 31,000 vehicles and 70,000 drivers working on a
regular basis.[1] This overcrowded and overcompetitive situation has made
it quite difficult for the medallion industry to remain financially solvent.
The gypsy competition in addition to the cost inefficiency of its operation
has put the medallion industry in danger of collapse.

   In particular, the rise in the number of non-medallion operators throughout the city has diminished the value of the medallion. The following graph
clearly shows that fleet medallions have steadily lost their black market
value with the rapid growth of the non-medallion industry.[2] This condition
points to the severe competition among the two industries and the relative
strength of the non-medallion operators in controlling major sectors of the
taxi empire.

Social Relations Between Gypsies and Medallions:
Open Warfare

To add to the medallion industry's problems the gypsy drivers have declared war on all medallion taxis. Not only have they been interested in
grabbing a larger share of the taxi market, they have been willing to resort
to violence to achieve their ends. Increasingly medallion taxi drivers are
being intimidated whenever they overstep their territorial boundaries and
find themselves on private livery and gypsy cab turf. Likewise, the medallion cab drivers are quick to pounce upon the gypsy driver who strays into
their territory. However, on home turf the gypsy and private livery are
supreme; neither the police nor the persistent medallion taxi driver have
been able to dislodge them from large sectors of the city.

   The inequities of medallioned taxi service in the ghettoes of New York
are no longer the problem; the gypsies have resolved that problem at the
expense of the negligent taxi industry. Instead of contending with accusa-

This gypsy driver works for the largest black livery in New York City. His amused look comes from knowing that rules or no rules, police or no police, his services are demanded and preferred in the black community. (Photograph by Mark Sherman)

tions of discrimination, the fleet owner and driver now face a larger crisis with the hoards of non-medallioned cabs swarming into territory that has traditionally been the bread and butter of the industry. The skirmish has turned into a battle and the medallioned cab driver no longer knows if he is on the winning side of the war.

The first major battle in the industry came in the summer of 1968 when 13 medallioned taxis were overturned and burned in Bedford Stuyvesant.[3] Since that time innumerable skirmishes have broken out throughout the city pitting the medallion taxi drivers against their ghetto enemies. During taxi strikes, the gypsy contingent has quickly flooded the streets with their vehicles in an effort to gain more of the market. Counter measures on the part of the medallion industry to drive out the illegal bandits have all too often met with failure.

Further warnings against the unwanted intrusion of medallion cabs took place during the summer of 1971 when over 100 cab windows were smashed and one taxi burned at a Bronx taxi fleet. These overt gestures of hostility toward the medallion empire have been quite effective deterrents to the presence of the medallion taxi.

The intimidating actions of non-medallioned cabs have secured them a permanent foothold within the transportation system of New York. In a

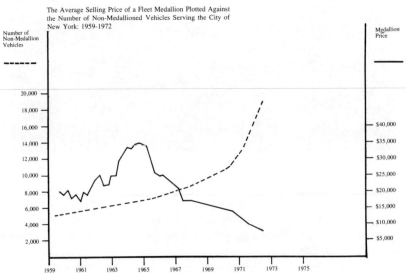

figure 9.1

The Average Selling Price of a Fleet Medallion Plotted Against the Number of Non-Medallioned Vehicles Serving the City of New York: 1959-1972

survey conducted in 1971 three out of four vehicles serving the poor residential areas of the city were gypsy cabs.[4] In addition, the gypsy cabs have established preeminence within the boroughs of Brooklyn and the Bronx as the primary form of taxi travel.[5] The medallion industry, on the other hand, has been forced to serve more limited and exclusive markets. Its service has become increasingly centered on the island of Manhattan and its clientele has been limited to middle and upper income residents.

The distinction between the two industries is radical. The gypsy cab is the poor man's alternative to the medallion cab. This distinction, however, has not deterred the gypsy drivers from gouging into traditional medallion territory. Like the taxi driver, gypsy drivers are out to grab all the money they can get. If this should mean infringing upon medallion territory, there is nothing to stop them, especially if the police are willing to desist from enforcing the law and the medallion drivers are unwilling to stand them off. This has left the city divided into separate warring states with the medallioned cabs garrisoned in the center of Manhattan and the gypsy operators in control of major sections of the surrounding boroughs.

With the prospects of continued violence, inadequate taxi service and unregulated fly-by-night gypsy operations, the city council at the insistence of Mayor Lindsay created the Taxi and Limousine Commission in March of 1971.[6]

The Public Interest: Taxi and Limousine Commission

The Taxi and Limousine Commission marks the third major legal transformation of the taxi industry. Unlike the original Taxicab Board of Control of the early thirties, the Taxi and Limousine Commission's implicit purpose has been to break up the medallion monopoly created by government cartel and reestablish a more equitable level of service for the entire city. To accomplish these aims, the commission has set forth a program for the supervision and regulation of the private livery industry.

The commission's first chairman, Michael J. Lazar, took the position that the private livery industry is in fact vested with public interest. In keeping with his position, he initially redefined the private livery as a public livery, maintaining that this would not allow these operators to engage in business upon the streets. Nevertheless, the willingness of the commission to license and regulate the private liveries has been viewed as a major turn of events within the industry. To the medallion industry, the possible regulation and licensing of the private liveries under the banner of a public livery status, is a direct threat to their investments, since it is generally acknowledged by all parties, including the commission, that there is no real distinction between a private livery and an illegal gypsy cab. As Mr. Lazar stated in October of 1972:

> I've come to the conclusion that any car operating outside of regulations has got to conduct himself like a gypsy. All a cop has to do is take notice long enough and the car is going to pick up along the street. I could pick up 30 violations in an hour of driving around.[7]

By this definition a program of regulating the private livery industry would be a step closer to the ultimate legitimation of the illegal street service provided by these vehicles.

In the midst of this confusion, the city council has denied the commission the power to regulate the private liveries as public liveries under the charter of the city. This has left the commission with its hands tied, since the commission has hinged its existence on the need for city supervision of the private liveries.

Lacking formal power to intervene in the transportation problems facing the black and Puerto Rican communities of the city the Taxi and Limousine Commission has had to rely on what little power they were granted under Local Law 12 under which the commission was created. The refusal of the city council to grant the commission the power to regulate private liveries, which has been partly reinforced by the political power of the fleet owners, virtually destroyed two Commissioners' plans to restore peace to the gypsy and taxi industries. However even though the Commission lacks enforcement power over the gypsies or the private liveries, it has suggested, in a tone of command, that all gypsies submit to regulation and licensing under the banner of "Limousine" status. This program, to no one's surprise, has barely received acceptance within the black and Puerto Rican communities of the city. For most operators the $100 licensing fee demanded by the commission offers little or no advantage over their present system of operation. At best the $100 license would be a means of promoting the integrity of the private livery in the ghetto areas or throughout the city where there is a demand for their services. The problem is that what little integrity they gained through municipal licensing would be offset by the stigma attached to municipal services in general and taxi service in particular. As Calvin Williams, owner of one of the largest black private livery outfits in the city and assemblyman from Bedford Stuyvesant said to the author:

> Why should I pay $100 to put Mike Lazar's name on my car? They (the gypsies) get nothing for their $100 and get nothing from the police or the Taxi and Limousine Commision. They just paid $100 to have their license revoked. It's such a ripoff.[8]

It is Williams' opinion that the Taxi and Limousine Commission is deliberately favoring the medallion interests and suppressing the private cab operators in an effort to eliminate them. This, he said, has been attempted through the procedure of police summonses issued by the commission for trivial infractions, which he states, "has no jurisdiction over us whatsoever. It's a form of harassment." Lacking real power, the commission is left with only the power to threaten the gypsies into line or out of existence. Obviously this has not stopped the gypsies or private liveries from continued operation.

The problem of harassment for the gypsy and private livery operators is somewhat more severe than mere municipal interference. The city's taxi fleet owners, according to Mr. Williams, have turned to gangland tactics to kill the continued growth of the big gypsy operators. He has stated, "I've had contracts put out on me. They're trying to get rid of me and when they do they get rid of the private cab."[9] Mr. Williams considers himself the central target of attack because as he told it, "I employ more black people than anyone else in the city of New York"—a statement he later modified by limiting his comparison exclusively to the black employers of New York. His position on the future of the private cab (he didn't talk about the gypsy because as he sees it that word is just the same as calling someone a red or a nigger) was clear; "if you kill the head the body dies."

Although Mr. Williams feels threatened by the political and underworld power of the taxi fleet owners, he is not altogether a babe in the woods. In 1968 he was indicted for the burning of several medallion taxis in Bedford Stuyvesant. This specific incident, more than any other, formalized the fleet owners and the fleet drivers' refusal to serve the ghettoes. Mr. Williams explained in 1973 that, "he took the rap" and received only a $250 fine for punishment just to get the taxi fleet owners off his back and dissipate some of the public resentment against private livery operators. His claim to innocence is reminiscent of Spiro Agnew's resignation speech but his power within the Bedford Stuyvesant area of Brooklyn makes his possible guilt a moot point.

Despite the obvious disadvantages of becoming regulated under the commission's authority as many as 2,000 vehicles were licensed in 1973 when the licensing program began.[10] These operators initially assumed that the commission's licensing program would offer them certain privileges which have traditionally belonged to the medallion cab. As a result of this misconception most livery operators began dropping out of the program once it became clear that the commission was not about to give them the privilege of picking up off the street. In fact the exodus has been so great that in 1975 a spokesman for the commission indicated that it would be a surprise if even 100 operators decided to renew their licenses for the coming year. Those few operators who are still willing to abide by the commission's rules are very much different than operators like Mr. Williams. They tend to be white operators from the suburban fringes of the city where little or no money is to be made from picking up passengers off the street. Since these operators make little or no money from illegal pickups they don't feel threatened by the thought of regulation.

The problem behind the Taxi and Limousine Commission's policies toward the private livery industry is that the commission has been more intent upon punishing this class of vehicles, despite its lack of authority over them, than developing ways of improving transportation for the general public that relies on these vehicles. The irony of the situation is that, "if a gypsy driver picks up off the street his license is revoked but if a medallion driver refuses to pick up off the street he is merely fined." The implicit position of the commission has been that it should assist the taxi industry against the onslaughts of the gypsies. However this policy has allied the commission with the inefficient taxi operators who still have strong political power within the city government but are no longer the best producers of service. By protecting the taxi interests, the commission is really resisting the positive advantages the gypsy and private livery operators are offering the public.

In theory a program to regulate the liveries would not be a threat to the medallion industry as long as the prohibition against cruising could be enforced. However this is an unrealizable dream since the gypsy industry will not surrender that option nor will it be intimidated by the increased use of police surveillance. The gypsy industry will apparently fight to the bitter end, hoping it can achieve the status of a medallioned taxi.

The Police Interest:Disinterest

The crux of the commission's problem is that an effective licensing program rests upon strong and continued police enforcement of the regulations. This, however, is something the police are unwilling and unable to do. Years of experience within the black and Puerto Rican communities of New York have made the police quite hesitant to enforce any laws which might, 1) instigate full scale riots, 2) destroy whatever rapport exists between themselves and the community and 3) increase the danger of their jobs. They have arrived at a tenuous compromise between the laws promulgated by the city and the state and the demands of the residents of the black and Puerto Rican communities. In effect the cops role has become one of a political mediator between the demands of the city government and the vested interests it represents, and the demands of the black and Puerto Rican communities. In this sense the laws are enforced but only in so far as they do not upset the relative order and stability of life within the ghetto.

Another important explanation of the police leniency on gypsy operators is that most cops in the ghetto are either black or Puerto Rican and are often snubbed by taxis while they are off the job. "They don't push private cab laws," says Williams, "because they're peeved at the taxis."

It is quite apparent from recent outbreaks of violence among gypsy drivers that they have no intentions of relinquishing any of the new found status they have received within the ghetto nor any of the territory formerly served by the taxi industry. In September and October of 1973 a series of riots erupted in the Bronx that served to give full warning to the police and the Taxi and Limousine Commission to stay away.

These riots and protests took on added importance far beyond any that had occurred before since they involved prominent political figures from the black and Puerto Rican communities of the city.

In one case assemblyman Armando Montano reacted to the commission's edict banning the use of taximeters by gypsy cabs (an edict which in fact had no legal validity) by provoking a riot among gypsy drivers attending a mass demonstration. The New York Times reported:

> Mr. Montano allegedly climbed on top of an auto and using a bullhorn, told the crowd of about 500 people to, "put the police on notice that there will be a bloodbath tonight." He was arrested a short time later when according to the police, he attempted to free a man they had detained on a charge of smashing the windows of a yellow medallion taxi.

This event along with a subsequent mass demonstration against police interference with the gypsy operators was ample warning that the police and the Taxi and Limousine Commission should leave well enough alone.

Perhaps the only point upon which the Taxi and Limousine Commission and the gypsies both agree is that Abe Beame is going to make it tough for the gypsies for the simple reason that he is deeply rooted in the medallion cab interests. The future of the gypsy and the effectiveness of the commission both depend upon the mayor's police policies. It is generaly acknowledged that Beame has favored a strong policy of law and order in the ghettoes and demanded an increased deployment of the police force in those areas where the gypsies thrive. This situation could make it difficult for the gypsies but it will not eliminate their continued growth. Perhaps the only difficulty will be for the police since they might find it difficult to alleviate ghetto problems through relaxed enforcement if the threat of being fired is weighed against the threat of being gunned down by gypsy drivers.

The importance of the gypsy cab in the city and its acceptance by large sectors of the city are strong reasons why it will prevail over any mayor's policies. Furthermore, anyone who is familiar with the trend toward increasing concentrations of blacks and Puerto Ricans in America's central cities can understand why black economics and specifically the gypsy cab industry might gain more power as the whites evacuate the central city.

In the few years since the commission has been in existence, major crises have developed. The most visible signs of danger have been the following: the decay of the union, the emigration of large sections of the taxi labor force to the gypsy industry, the growth of the illegal gypsy empire and the persistent and often violent refusal of gypsy operators to submit to any licensing and regulations the commission has asked them to accept.

The emergence of the gypsy industry appears to be the final chapter in the history of the medallion empire. The threat of a gypsy take-over of the city has weakened the medallion monopoly and crumbled the precarious labor structure of the industry. Rather than uniting in opposition to the gypsy take-over, large numbers of drivers are joining the enemy.

In fact, the bigger the gypsy empire has become, the more enticing it has been for a fleet driver to abandon his profession and go into business for himself. This is the latest version of the old battle between the fleet driver and the owner. The owners' fear of off-the-meter negotiators has been replaced by his fear of being run out of business by fleet drivers who have entered the gypsy industry. These former taxi drivers now account for as many as 40 percent of all the gypsies on the streets.

As a final means of averting the financial ruin of the industry at the hands of the gypsies, many fleet owners have begun to liquidate their assets. This has been accomplished through the sale of large numbers of fleet medallions to small entrepreneurs under the banner of the two car taxi fleet. These mini fleets as they are called have emerged from the remains of over a dozen major fleets that have been liquidated over the last two years. Since 1973 over 1,600 fleet medallions have been turned into two car fleets selling for prices as high as $18,500 in the open market. Not surprisingly the mini fleet concept has boosted the value of the fleet medallion since it has offered prospective buyers the chance of acquiring two medallions for nearly the same price as one owner driver medallion. This development has allowed many of the inefficient taxi fleets to drop out of the industry without going bankrupt.

The liquidation of ten New York fleets in September of 1971 was the first clear indication of the instability of the industry. Since that time many other large fleets have begun selling off their medallions in order to take advantage of the windfall profits created by the mini fleet concept. This development has tended to promote the breakup of the large taxi fleets making it less profitable for a fleet owner to maintain his fleet than to sell it off. The implications for the public are clear: without effective legal and political action by the city council and the Taxi and Limousine Commission, the days of safe and inexpensive taxi service as provided by the large New York fleets appear to be numbered.

10

Conclusion

The taxi industry is perhaps the best example of an industry in the early stages of laissez-faire capitalism. In this regard it has been most preoccupied with establishing monopolistic controls over the market, because there are no effective means for controlling service. A taxi ride is a one shot affair making all competitors equal in status, since the value of the service is established through its immediacy and not through the supplier's ability to control the service. Since a taxi ride is an intangible consumer product there is no way the owner can stockpile his services and consequently no way he can maintain an effective monopoly over the market. To compensate for the vicissitudes of the market, taxi owners in New York City have used the power of municipal government to eliminate their competitors. This has been accomplished through legislation or police enforcement and led to the growth of an enormously valuable monopoly. In this fashion the industry's development over the past century can be understood in terms of attempts to stabilize the predicaments of a free enterprise system.

Municipal legislation tacitly allowed the medallion to become a highly valued commodity. However the fleet medallion, once valued at $35,000 has fallen prey to the open competition of the gypsy. In 1972 the medallion lay virtually forsaken on the streets of New York with one fleet owner claiming, "we can't even give them away." As of the fall of 1972 fleet medallions sold for as low as $6,000 for those willing to enter the business.[1] Ironically at that time the low price of fleet medallions deterred entrance into the business since the medallion no longer reflected economic opportunity.[2] Since 1972 the medallion has recovered some of its former value rising in price to $14,000 in 1973 and then to $18,500 in 1975. The recent increase reflects the creation of the two car mini fleets as well as a general industry wide realization that the commission is not intending to regulate or bring the gypsy on a parity with the medallion cab.

While the fleet medallion has risen in value as a result of the two car fleets the large fleet owners are still involved in a competitive business without the economic advantages of the gypsy cabs. Much of their disadvantage has been caused by unpaid medallion loans, which in 1971 had unpaid balances of approximately $8,400 per cab and were being paid back at an interest rate of 11 percent.[3] This cost inefficiency accelerated the decline of the fleet owner and enticed the private liveries to serve as surrogate taxis. In this way the medallion monopoly caused its own decline.

Public service has been improved with the growth of the gypsy cab operators although their presence has not eliminated the cost inefficiency of the fleet owner or his low regard for the public. The immorality and corruption reflected in the industry's attitude toward the public has been exacerbated by the political acquiescence of one city administration after another. In fact the only positive reformations of taxi service in New York have come illegally. Lindsay's willingness to break the law in the early days of his reign as mayor was primarily responsible for the downfall of the medallion monopoly—the consequences of which have been improved service to the ghettoes and all the outlying boroughs of the city.

Lindsay's actions reflect the same illegality as those of the driver "beating the system." Unable to reform the city's taxi service through legislation, Lindsay allowed the gypsy industry to blossom overnight, sweeping into control of major sectors of New York. Although the city administration tacitly allowed the illegal gypsy to become an integral part of the urban transportation system of New York, it has refused to license or regulate these operators. This kind of scandalous political behavior has caused the bitter competition between the gypsy and the taxi to turn to violence.

The city administration has placed itself in a precarious position; on the one side they are using the power of government to favor specific private interests within the taxi industry and on the other they are breaking these laws in order to alleviate some of the more blatant inequities of taxi service in the ghettoes of New York.

The taxi industry unlike any other public service is one of the most visible and critical services in the city. Millions of people come into contact with New York and New Yorkers everyday through the person of the cab driver. Because of his close contact with visitors, foreigners and New Yorkers, his actions reflect not only on himself but on the city of New York and its style of life. In this sense the taxi driver is an ambassador of public relations establishing a vital link between the city and all of its visitors. If he does not choose to act honestly the public is forever at his mercy.

The city administration must take steps to improve taxi service. This issue is not, "who is to profit from municipal legislation," it is, "how is the public to be served better for less cost?" Service will improve only when municipal government comprehends that the quality of taxi service in New York is an integral component of the general quality of life. So far private interests and public government have expressed an appalling lack of responsibility for the nature of taxi service, for its quality as well as its quantity.

The quality of service provided by the medallion taxi has not been improved despite the creation of the Taxi and Limousine Commission. Although this commission was created in order to eliminate the concept of the medallion and bring gypsy operators under city regulation, so far it has done virtually nothing. Like many other branches of the New York city administration, the Taxi and Limousine Commission is staffed with political hacks and incompetent bureaucrats who have padded the agency with unnecessary and inexperienced people. Ask any cab driver his opinion of the commission and most will say, "It hasn't done any good and it isn't going to do any good." Like the Taxicab Board of Control under Mayor Jimmy Walker, the Taxi and Limousine Commission appears to be fated for extinction. However in this case it is not the smell of graft but the incompetence of bureaucracy that will lead to its removal.

Regardless of the problems of municipal government, the gypsy cab operators must be regulated in order to protect the public. As many as a million people are using their services daily without the assurance that these are honest men, reliable vehicles or legal rates of fare. Similarly the city must eliminate the concept of the medallion and develop an industry that provides public service at a reasonable cost. There is no reason why the city of New York should have allowed the fleet owners the right to raise their fares to double the price of a taxi ride in 1967. It is to the interest of the public to eliminate the medallion monopoly if it wishes to receive better service at a cheaper cost.

Another means to improve service to the public is to improve the working conditions of the driver. Only when cheating and discrimination are no longer needed by the driver as tools of his trade will the public be treated fairly.

Although the cheaters of the industry are often the scapegoats of fleet owners, the public and politicians, their existence is merely a manifestation of the larger economic structure of the industry, the corruption of municipal government, and the underworld affairs of unions operating within the industry. These parties are all responsible for the underlying problems of taxi service in New York. The poor hack driver finds himself victimized by his wage contract, and regulated and supervised unlike any other profession of equal status. He is blamed for much of the problem when in fact the problem has been created under the sanction of municipal legislation.

The gypsy cab industry also has been used as a public scapegoat by the same parties who have condemned the actions of the cab driver. However the existence of the gypsy cab has forced the industry to redefine its business rules and adapt to a changing economic world. For the fleet driver this has meant the opportunity of becoming a gypsy cab driver and for the fleet owner it has meant the necessity of reducing his cost inefficiency.

Owner-drivers have not realized the extent to which the situation has been redefined by the gypsy cab industry. This is reflected in the extreme short-sightedness of owner-drivers who have bought their medallions in the last few years for as high as $32,000 while gypsy operators have entered the field without any economic restrictions at all. These men are still living in another age, unaware of the economics of the times or of the true impact of the gypsy cab industry upon the value of the $32,000 investment. The owner-driver's investment in an overinflated medallion, at a time when the police and municipal government have relaxed their surveillance of the gypsy cabs, reflects a misguided faith in the politicians at city hall. Some of these men have paid up to $50,000 including interest on the medallion loan with the hope that municipal government will protect their extravagant investment.

As the gypsy expands from a ghetto service to a metropolitan service more individuals will become attracted to entering the gypsy industry than to buying owner-driver medallions. Up to this point the owner-drivers have remained nearly all white, and the gypsy drivers nearly all black or Puerto Rican. However, as the gypsy empire expands or becomes legalized within the Charter of the City of New York, the racial barrier separating the two industries will dissolve and white drivers will turn to the gypsy cab as the alternative to buying an overvalued medallion. The gypsy in this sense represents the promise of the future—bringing economic opportunity for the poor and better service to the public.

Notes

Introduction

1. *New York Times,* "Taximeters Would Stop Extortion by Cabmen" August 9, 1906.
2. Memoranda in the matter of Issuing of Licenses Relating to Street Trades and Personal Service, 1913, page 8, Department of Licenses.
3. *Ibid.,* page 6.
4. Laws and Ordinances of the Corporation of the City of New York, 1834, Chapter I, Title VI, Of Special Hackney Coaches or Carriages, pages 15–16.
5. *Taxi Weekly,* "Terminal Enters Market: Takes Over Yellow Taxicab Concession at Penn Station," February 10, 1930.
6. See the glossary for a short dictionary of the drivers' language.
7. *Ibid.*
8. Police Department, City of New York, Rules Governing Drivers of Public Taxicabs and Public Coaches, January 1971, pages 1–101.
9. See the glossary on drivers' language.

Chapter 1

1. In this context I am using Lewis Coser's use of the word "irrational" as he develops it in "The Functions of Social Conflict." An action is irrational if it is not the most direct and effective means of achieving one's end. In this case, the implication is that the drivers' cheating is less effective and a less convincing means of negotiating with the fleet owner than union sponsored collective bargaining. Unfortunately, the rational approach to making a living in the New York taxi industry has fallen by the wayside, because of the inherent difficulties involved in unionization and collective bargaining. This problem is the focus of Chapters 4 and 5 which deal with the historical problems of unionizing New York's taxi drivers.

2. Michael Lazar, The Non-Medallion Industry: A Transportation Phenomena, City Record Supplement, November 19, 1971, Appendix F.

3. Police Department Memo, Mandatory Installation of Partitions in Taxicabs, September 3, 1968.

4. Harry M. Perry, Taximeter Motor Cabs in America, *Scientific American,* November 9, 1907, pages 327–329.

5. Police Department Memo, Mandatory Installation of Partitions in Taxicabs, September 3, 1968.

6. Interview with a taxi driver in the month of August 1971.

7. Spiegelman, Jack, "Confession of a New York Cabbie," *New York Magazine,* February 21, 1971.

8. A survey of 400 fleet taxi drivers was conducted by the author in the summer of 1971. These 400 drivers included drivers from all the major taxi garages in the four major boroughs of the city. The results of the survey are, to say the least, startling. New Yorkers have long mistrusted the character of the New York hack; however, nobody has ever gone so far as to corner the cab driver into a voluntary admission and justification of his unethical practices.

9. *Ibid.*

10. *Ibid.*11. *Ibid.*

12. Many people are unperturbed by the breakdown of ethics among the younger generation, perhaps because of its epidemic proportions. However when we, the public, realize that the elders of our society are engaging in some of the same practices, cheating can no longer be considered deviant behavior.

13. See footnote 8.

14. *Ibid.*15. *Ibid.*16. *Ibid.*

17. *New York Times,* "Taximetre Cabs in Service," October 2, 1907.

18. *Scientific American,* "Taximeter Frauds," October 21, 1911, pages 260–261.

19. Fast meters are a major problem in the gypsy cab industry. As many as one out of three gypsy operators using a meter operates above the advertised rate. This was disclosed in private interviews with the Taxi and Limousine Commission during the summer of 1971.

20. *New York Times,* December 20, 1968, "New Meters Bar Cab's Cheating."

21. *Ibid.*22. Correspondence between an anonymous cab driver and the author.

23. *Scientific American,* "Taximeter Frauds," October 21, 1911, pages 260–261.

24. New York Times, October 30, 1956, "Police Lift Ban on 'No' of Home Bound Cabby."

25. Spring 3100, *The Magazine for Policeman,* "Taxicab Truck Surveillance Unit," March 1971; Police Department, City of New York, *Rules Governing Drivers of Public Taxicabs and Public Coaches,* January 1971.

26. Interview with hack bureau representatives, December 1970.

27. Charles Vidich, *Service Refusal in the Taxi Industry,* City Record Supplement, October 28, 1971, pages 44–45.

28. *Ibid.*

29. Hack police convey a certain fondness of feeling for the super hustler when discussing their activities. In several interviews conducted during the summer of 1971 the author noted the interest of the hack police in recounting the best hustles they had seen.

Chapter 2

1. Nelson, Jeffrey P., "Group Riding and Central Dispatch," City Record Supplement, October 28, 1971, pages 367–368.

2. Katz, Stanley B., "Citizen Complaint Hearing Procedures," City Record Supplement, October 28, 1971, page 402.

3. *Ibid.,* page 403.

4. *Ibid.,* page 420.

5. *Ibid.,* page 421.

6. *Ibid.,* page 403.

7. *Ibid.,* page 403.

Chapter 3

1. *New York Times,* "To Run Electric Cabs," May 7, 1897.

2. *Scientific American,* "The Electric Cab Service of New York City, March 25, 1899.

3. *Scientific American,* "An Electric Hansom," March 13, 1897.

4. Adams, Alton D., "Cost and Limitations of Electric Vehicle Traction," *Scientific American,* July 28, 1900.

5. *Scientific American,* "The Electric Cab Service of New York City," March 25, 1899.

6. *The Horseless Age,* July 1900.

7. *the Taxi Weekly,* "To Give New Taxi for Information on Old Electric Cab," October 1, 1928.

8. *New York Times,* October 2, 1907.

9. Department of Licenses, Mayor's Office 1914–1924.

10. The present relative of the early horse drawn carriage can still be found at Central Park South, offering tours of the Park to those able to afford its services.

11. City Record, May 27, 1913, pages 555–564, and the case of Yellow Taxicab vs. Gaynor, November 1913.

12, Yellow Taxicab Co. vs. Gaynor, Supreme Court, special term, New York County, August 21, 1913.

13. City Record, May 27, 1913, page 556.

14. *New York Times,* May 28, 1928 "Taxicab Ordinance Passes by 65 to 1," and the case of Yellow Taxicab vs. Gaynor, Supreme Court, special term, New York County, August 21, 1913.

15. *Ibid.*

16. New York City Ordinances, approved November 15, 1917.

17. *New York Times,* August 7, 1913, "Calls Taxicab Law Financial Murder," and *New York Times,* November 7, 1915, "Two Taxi Branches Close," and November 8, 1915, "U.S. Motor Cab Co. Quits."

18. Yellow Taxicab vs. Gaynor, Supreme Court, special term, New York County, August 21, 1913, page 302.

19. *Ibid.*

20. City Record, May 27, 1913, pages 555–564.

21. *New York Times,* February 4, 1923 "New York's 15,000 Cruising Taxis Make City Unsafe—Tie Up Traffic," also Annual Report of the Department of Licenses of the Mayor's Office for 1920.

22. *New York Times,* July 22, 1924, "Taxicab Companies Begin A Rate War."

23. *New York Times,* July 23, 1924 "Taxi Rates Are Cut to 10 Cents a Half Mile."

24. *New York Times,* August 3, 1924, "Taxicab War Absorbs City."

25. *New York Times,* February 22, 1925, "Taxi Evils—McAdoo and Enright Prescribe."

26. *Ibid.*

27. *Ibid.*

28. *New York Times,* February 1925.

29. New York City Code of Ordinances, March 1925, Chapter 14, pages 338–347.

30. Police Annual Reports for 1925–1930.

31. Report of the Mayor's Commission on Taxicabs, September 23, 1930, pages 8–10.

32. *New York Times,* January 30, 1932, "Taxi Control Law Signed by Walker."

33. *New York Times,* May 13, 1932, "Walker Got $26,535 Bonds from J. A. Sisto as 'gift', Taxi Financier Testifies," page 12, also "The Insolence of Office: The Story of the Seabury Investigations," page 262.

34. *New York Times,* May 8, 1932, "Text of Seabury's Address in Washington, D.C.," page 24.

35. *New York Times,* August 23, 1932, "Witnesses Defend Mayor on Taxi Law, Denying Favoritism or Monopoly Plan; Wont Block Governor, Court Indicates."

36. *New York Times,* May 13, 1932, "Walker Got $26,535 Bonds from J. A. Sisto . . ." page 12.

37. *New York Times,* December 5, 1932, "Tammany Yields to Banker's Demands; Drastic Pay Cuts, Abolition of 3 Boards Among Reforms Up for Adoption Today," page 1.

38. New York City Ordinances, Haas Act, City Record No. 99, adopted March 9, 1937, page 37.

39. *Ibid.*

40. Report of the Mayor's Commission on Taxicabs, September 23, 1930, page 17.

41. Report of the Mayor's Committee on Taxicab Survey to Honorable Fiorello H. La Guardia.

42. *Ibid.,* page 5.

43. Survey of Owner Drivers conducted in July of 1971.

44. Teller vs. Clear Service Co., Supreme Court, Pretrial Term, New York County, Part I, March 6, 1958, page 186.

45. Approximately 58% of all accidents involve personal injury to the passenger or pedestrians and 42% of the accidents involve no more than property damage. The danger of personal injury is quite likely in a taxi accident. Moreover, taxi accidents have increased dramatically in the last few years over the decade of the fifties. The annual volume of taxi accidents during the 1950s was as follows:
1955 — 6,506
1956 — 5,676
1957 — 6,260
1958 — 6,579
1959 —7,172
1960 — 6,575
1970 — 16,368 includes fleet owned taxi accidents only
1971— 13,556.

46. See the following chapter on the union and the heterogeneity of membership.

47. Teller vs. Clear Service Co., Supreme Court, Pretrial Term, New York County, Part I, March 6, 1958, page 188.

48. *Ibid.,* page 190.

49. Mull vs. Colt Co. Inc., United States district court, Southern District, New York, 1962, page 48.

50. *Ibid.*

Chapter 4

1. Many of the large fleets were collapsing because of the reduced rates instituted in 1913. In addition, the union played a central role in leading some of the early fleets to bankruptcy. See the *New York Times* of November 7 and 8, 1915. The low rates and the union demands proved to be the downfall of three major New York fleets.

2. *New York Times,* November 6, 1913, Threaten Taxicab Strike, November 6, 1915, "800 Taxi Chauffeurs Called Out on Strike."

3. *New York Times,* January 12, 1917, "Taxicab Company Wrecked by Strike."

4. *Ibid.*

5. *New York Times, February 14, 1920, "To Organize Chauffeurs."*

6. *New York Times,* November 18, 1922, "1,000 Black and White Chauffeurs Are Out."

7. *New York Times,* August 23, 1923, "800 Taxi Drivers Vote to Strike."

8. *New York Times, March 7, 1925, "Taxi Men See Hylan, But His Side Wins."*

9. *New York Times,* May 10, 1928, "Taxi Drivers Organize" and August 26, 1928, "Taxi Drivers Form Union."

10. *New York Times,* February 3, 1934, "12,000 Cabs Off Streets in Strike Over City Tax: La Guardia Aids Drivers."

11. *Ibid.*

New York Times, February 9, 1934, "Taxi Strike Ends."

13. *Ibid.*

14. *New York Times,* March 10, 1934, "Labor Board Seeks Taxi Strike Peace."

15. *New York Times,* March 24, 1934, "Sinister Forces Balk Taxi Peace, Deutsch Charges."

16. *New York Times,* April 5, 1938, "$1,000,000 Racket in Taxicabs Bared as 5 Are Indicted" and July 14, 1934, "Luciana Aide Held in Taxicab Racket."

17. *The Taxi Weekly,* April 9, 1938, "Dewey Exposes Taxi Racket."

18. *New York Times,* August 13, 1939, "Lepke a Gang Leader Who Liked His Privacy."

19. *The Taxi Weekly,* April 9, 1938, "Dewey Exposes Taxi Racket."

20. *New York Times,* April 5, 1938, "$1,000,000 Racket in Taxicabs Bared as 5 Are Indicted."

21. *Ibid.*

22. Hearing on Code of Fair Practices and Competition, National Industrial Recovery Administration, February 12–14, 1934, New York City.

23. Police Annual Report, 1931, The City of New York.

24. *New York Times,* May 30, 1937.

25. *New York Times,* June 1, 1937, "A.F.L. Taxi Union Threatens Strike."

26. *New York Times,* July 6, 1937, "Single C.I.O. Union to Cover Transit."

27. *New York Times,* June 12, 1937, "C.I.O. IS Victor in First Taxi Poll."

28. *New York Times,* August 11, 1937, "C.I.O. Wins the Poll of Parmalee Drivers."

29. *New York Times,* August 31, 1937, "Taxicab Strike is Threatened in Row Over C.I.O. Closed Shop."

30. *New York Times,* December 9, 1937, "New Taxi Compact Raises Men's Pay."

31. *New York Times,* December 24, 1937, "4 Big Taxi Fleets Sign with the C.I.O."

32. *New York Times,* February 28, 1938, "Two Taxi Groups Cut Pay of 10,000 Drivers, Renounce Union Contract; Strike Is Feared."

33. *Ibid.* 34. *New York Times,* January 6, 1939, Outcome Divided in Taxi Elections."

35. *Ibid.*

36. *New York Times,* October 24, 1946, "New Lewis Union For Taxi Drivers."

37. *New York Times,* January 27, 1947, "TWU to Start Taxi Drive."

38. *New York Times,* April 26, 1947, "Union Charter Revoked."

39. *New York Times,* March 31, 1949, "Taxi Drivers Fear Violence; Most Queried Oppose Strike."

40. *New York Times, April 7, 1949, "Union 'Releases' Owner-Run Taxis; Strike's End Seen."*

41. *New York Times,* May 5, 1949, "Teamsters Union Woos Taxi Drivers."

42. In 1939, after several years of factional rivalry, a split occurred in the ranks of the growing United Automobile Workers Union of the C.I.O. One section of the Union broke off and was chartered by the A.F.L. under the same name as the Union with which its members had previously been affiliated—The United Automobile Workers A.F.L. The UAW-AFL was actually larger than the UAW-CIO during the late thirties; however, the strength of the former soon dwindled. At the time of the taxi organizing drive in the early fifties, the UAW-AFL had no more than 80,000 members and had completely dropped out of union activities in the automobile manufacturing industries.

43. *New York Times,* October 3, 1952, "Flash Strike Halts Hundreds of Taxis."

44. *New York Times,* June 27, 1952, "Taxi Fares and Pay of Judges Raised by Estimate Board,"

45. Senate Report No. 1417, 85th Congress, "Report of the Select Committee on Improper Activities in Labor or Management Field," page 163.

46. *Ibid.,* page 165.

47. *Ibid.,* page 165.

48. *Ibid.,* page 165.

49. *Ibid.,* page 173.

50. *Ibid.,* page 167.

51. *Ibid.,* page 173 and 218.

52. *Ibid.,* page 186.

53. *New York Times,* June 2, 1956, "Cab Driver's Union to Quit Business."

54. *Ibid.*

55. *The Enemy Within,* by Robert Kennedy.

56. Report of the Select Committee on Improper Activities in the Labor or Management Field, page 188.

57. *Ibid.,* page 199.

58. *New York Times,* January 19, 1956, "Cab Tie-Up Called 'Fizzle,' Success."

59. *New York Times,* August 1, 1957, "Hoffa is Linked to Dio in Scheme to Control Port."

60. *Ibid.*

61. *New York Times,* March 2, 1956, "Cabbie is Attacked by Crowd of 50."

62. *Ibid.*

63. *New York Times,* October 5, 1957, "Text of Hoffa is Address of Acceptance."

64. *New York Times.*

65. *The Taxi Weekly* of 1960.

Chapter 5

1. *New York Times,* July 18, 1962, "Taxi Drivers Forming Union."

2. *New York Times,* September 15, 1964, "Union of Cabbies Backed by Mayor."

3. *Ibid.*

4. *The Organization of Local 3036, New York City Taxi Union, AFL-CIO* by John O'Connor, summer of 1966, pages 12–13.

5. *Ibid.,* page 14.

6. *Ibid.,* page 15.

7. *New York Times,* June 16, 1965, "75% of Taxi Men Ballot on Union."

8. *New York Times,* July 2, 1965, "Police Add 1,400 in Taxi Violence."

9. *The Organization of Local 3036, New York City, Taxi Union, AFL-CIO* by John O'Connor, page 20.

10. *New York Times,* July 22, 1965, "22 Garages Vote for Taxi Union."

11. *New York Times,* May 25, 1966, "Cabbies Awarded $4.50 a Week More in Lindsay Ruling."

12. *New York Times,* November 22, 1967, "Cab Negotiations Go On, but Wildcat Strikes Begin."

13. This procedure was eliminated in May of 1969.

14. Service Refusal in the Taxi Industry (interim report) August 23, 1971 by Charles Vidich.

15. Based on an interview with Lt. Warner of the Police Department's hack bureau in July of 1971.

16. Police Annual Reports 1925 through 1971 and the Annual Report of the Department of Licenses of the Mayor's Office for the years 1914 to 1924.

17. Report of the Mayor's Committee on Taxicabs Survey to Honorable Fiorello H. La Guardia, June 28, 1934, page 9.

18. *New York Times,* December 21, 1970, "Taxis Return to Streets as Cabbies Approve Pact."

19. *The Hot Seat,* September, 1973.

20. *Ibid.*

21. National Labor Relations Board, Region 29, Carrick Service Corp. *et al.* etc. Employer and Taxi Drivers Organizing Committee AFL-CIO, petitioner, November 16, 1965, Appendix B.

22. *New York Times,* December 16, 1970, "2 Strikers Arrested in Brawl over Gypsy Cabs."

Chapter 6

1. Police Department memo of 1967, Division of Licenses, the Hack Bureau.
2. *New York Times,* May 29, 1966, "Cabbies Awarded $4.50 a Week More in Lindsay Ruling," page 1.
3. Applicants for hack licenses often waited for three months before they were processed through the Police Department's Hack Bureau.
4. Police Department memo of 1967 and interviews with various owners.
5. Police Annual Reports 1950 through 1971, Division of Licenses, the Hack Bureau.
6. New York City Ordinances of 1899, 1913, 1925, 1952, 1964, 1968, 1971; also the *New York Times,* August 3, 1924.
7. Records of the Police Department's Hack Bureau.
8. *Ibid.*
9. Memorandum of the Metropolitan Taxi Board of Trade, "Directory of Member Taxicab Garages," July 27, 1970.
10. Yellow Taxicab Co. vs. Gaynor, Appellate Division, First Department, November 1913, page 894.
11. A "hot seat" is a pressure sensitive device installed within the passenger seat of the taxi used to detect the presence of a passenger. The use of "hot seats" was felt to be the owner's long awaited solution to the driver practice of stealing money, since the "hot seat" automatically turns on the meter regardless of the desires of the driver.
12. The Taxi and Limosine Commission, Annual Report for 1972, page 9.
13. Berenyi, John, Effects of Taxi Strike, December 18, 1970.
14. Report of the Mayor's Committee on Taxicabs Survey to Honorable Fiorello H. La Guardia, June 28, 1934, page 11.

Chapter 7

1. Michael Lazar, "The Non-Medallion Industry: A Transportation Phenomena," City Record Supplement, November 19, 1971, Appendix F.
2. Charles Vidich, "Service Refusal in the Taxi Industry," City Record Supplement, October 28, 1971, pages 28-36.
3. *Ibid.*
4. *Ibid.*
5. *Ibid.*
6. Price Waterhouse & Co. *New York City Fleet Taxicab Industry: Financial Survey,* September 1967, and *New York City Fleet Taxicab Industry: Financial Survey,* June 30, 1970.

7. City Commission on Human Rights, *Public Hearing: The Investigation of Discriminatory Practices in the Taxicab Industry, 1966.*

8. Monthly Report of The Crime Analysis Division of the New York Police Department.

9. Correspondence of Oscar Katz to Michael Lazar, June 30, 1971, concerning owner driver use of partitions.

10. Interview with a Queens cab driver in July of 1971.

11. Ibid.

12. Monthly Report of the Crime Analysis Division of the New York Police Department.

13. Charles Vidich, "Service Refusal in the Taxi Industry," October 28, 1971, City Record Supplement, page 46.

Chapter 8

1. Robert Starr, "The Decline and Decline of New York," *New York Times Magazine,* November 21, 1971, page 62.

2. *Ibid.*

3. *Ibid.*

4. Charles Vidich, "Service Refusal in the Taxi Industry," October 28, 1971, City Record Supplement, page 19.

5. Oscar Ornati, *Transportation Needs of the Poor: A Case Study of New York.* Praeger Publishers, 1969, pages 39–46.

6. Michael Lazar, "The Non-Medallion Industry: A Transportation Phenomena," City Record Supplement, November 19, 1971, page 23.

7. Tri-State Transportation Commission, *Who Rides Taxis: A Regional Profile.* Volume 1, Number 11, February 1969.

8. Oscar Ornati, *Transportation Needs of the Poor: A Case Study of New York.* Praeger Publishers, 1969, page 30.

9. Michael Lazar, "The Non-Medallion Industry: A Transportation Phenomena," City Record Supplement, November 19, 1971, page 23.

10. *Ibid.*

11. *Ibid.*

12. *Ibid.*

13. Metropolitan Taxi Board of Trade, *Gypsy Cabs,* January 4, 1971, Memorandum to the Industry.

14. Metropolitan Taxi Board of Trade, *Gypsy Cabs,* January 4, 1971, Memorandum to the Industry.

15. Survey Conducted by the Author in July and August of 1971.

16. Memo to Deputy Commissioner in Charge of Legal Matters, *Proposed Changes in Administrative Code Re Taxicabs,* June 26, 1963.

17. *Ibid.*

18. *Ibid.*

19. *Ibid.*

20. Taxi and Limousine Commission, *Mandatory Penalties,* July 19, 1971.

21. Enoch Meningal, *The Interboro Public Livery Coalition, The Other Voice,* February 4, 1971, page 5.

Chapter 9

1. Michael Lazar, "The Non-Medallion Industry: A Transportation Phenomena," November 19, 1971, City Record Supplement.

2. The Taxi and Limousine Commission estimates that there are as many as 13,700 non-medallioned vehicles serving the city of New York. If this is true, then the gypsy has achieved a greater size than the medallion industry which is limited by law to 13,566 taxis.

3. *New York Times,* July 9, 1968, "Cabs are burned by Gypsy Drivers."

4. Michael Lazar, "The Non-Medallion Industry: A Transportation Phenomena," City Record Supplement, November 19, 1971, Appendix D.

5. *Ibid.,* Appendix K.

6. City Council of New York, *Local Law No. 12,* March 2, 1971, pages 1–4.

7. Frank J. Prial, "Taxi Industry Beset by Problems Looks for Ways to Stay on Duty," *New York Times,* page 82, October 17, 1972.

8. Interview with Calvin Williams on October 16, 1973

9. *Ibid.*

10. Interview with Abe Silver, Public Relations Director of the Taxi and Limousine Commission, on October 15, 1973.

11. New York Times. September 16, 1972, "Montano Paroled on Riot Charges."

Chapter 10

1. Interview with Nathan Levine, President of Bell System, November 28, 1972.

2. Over the past thirty years an average of 700 to 1,200 medallions were sold annually. In 1971 there were only 313 medallion sales within the industry—the lowest number of sales witnessed since the passage of the Haas Act limiting the number of taxis in New York.

3. Price Waterhouse & Co., *New York City Fleet Taxicab Industry: Financial Survey,* June 30, 1970, page 4.

Glossary

airport rats A phrase used to describe those drivers who habitually hustle at one or both of the New York airports.

bandits Anyone who steals from the passenger or the fleet owner.

bad actors A fleet owner phrase used to describe cheating drivers. He is a bad actor because he is not acting right.

bonus pay A monetary stimulus provided by the fleet owner to stabilize his work force and maintain the allegiance of his drivers. By paying the driver a bonus every three months, the fleet owner assuages the inequities of the labor contract.

bookings The proceeds of the money made off the meter. It is called bookings because drivers are required to book every trip made in a log as proof of their labor.

booking quota A measure designed to force drivers to make a specified amount of money per day or face the possibility of dismissal.

break the ice The first fare of the day. Usually this phrase is associated with getting a big fare at the airport to give the day a good push in the direction of making money.

buckers An old word used to describe drivers who attempted to "buck" into closed taxi lines in front of profitable terminals or hotels. Since most closed lines are controlled by fleet operators buckers usually implied that the driver owned his cab.

buggy Another name for a taxicab. The word is a holdover from the horse-drawn carriage days at the turn of the century.

bussing The violation of picking up passengers like a bus (and often from bus stands) and charging the meter rate to each party involved.

cattle boats from Puerto Rico A taxi driver's phrase used to describe the illegal gypsy operations in the ghettoes of New York. The implication of the phrase is that Puerto Rican automobiles, like Puerto Rican families, are overloaded with people.

common whore This is a union expression for scab labor. Generally these drivers are more concerned with making a buck than with the solidarity of the union.

crashing The attempt to break into the front of a live hack line. This practice is a clear example of the driver's willingness to cheat on his own brotherhood in order to make a living.

crooked dollar A phrase used by cab drivers as a description of the fleet owner, due to his sordid business operations and unethical labor practices. It was commonly used during the thirties when corruption was supreme.

cruising This is the common procedure for searching for fares. Cruising is perhaps a bit more common among fleet drivers than owner drivers since the former are not required to pay for the gasoline whereas the latter must pay for it out of their own pocket.

dead-heading Whenever a driver returns empty from the location he dropped off his last fare, it is described as dead-heading or heading back dead. Drivers attempt to reduce the amount of dead-heading by refusing long trips outside the heart of Manhattan.

dirty dollar see crooked dollar.

dock rats Those drivers that hustle incoming ships at New York's piers. Dock rats often negotiate with the stevedores to do dry runs (luggage without a passenger) operating like a U-Haul truck. By doing this, the driver does not have to account for the extra money he makes from delivering large trunks, since there is no visible sign to the hack police that business is being conducted if there is no one in the back seat. The practice of expressage of luggage was widely practiced in the days before the advent of the airplane.

doubling up The practice of putting more than one party in the same taxi and charging each party the price of the meter. This violation is extremely common at LaGuardia and Kennedy International Airport where large demands for taxi service often allow the driver the opportunity to chisel more than his share of business.

expressage The act of carrying bags or articles within the taxi without an accompanying passenger. This was prevalent during the days when ocean liners reigned as the number one form of transatlantic travel.

fare rate The schedule of cost determined through units of distance and time. The fare rate schedule is posted on the outside of each taxi. The present fare rate is 60 cents for the first 1/5 mile and 10 cents for each additional 1/5 mile with 10 cents for each 72 seconds of waiting time.

flag The lever or arm used to activate the meter of the taxicab.

flag down no passenger This is a violation most commonly used by owner drivers as a technique of raising the initial drop of the meter. By allowing the meter to run without a passenger in the taxicab, the driver can extort a higher price for the ride without the passenger knowing. Often drivers will obscure the meter so that the passenger is not aware of the swindle. Fleet drivers never practice this technique since everything recorded on the meter is shared with the owner. Owner drivers, operating for themselves, are not curtailed by the presence of the meter. Aside from its use to extort money, this technique can be used to refuse service to a passenger going to an undesirable location. "I'm sorry, sir, but I've already been hired."

flag up This is the number one violation of the industry. It describes the practice of leaving the flag of the meter up, in the off position, while the driver proceeds to steal the owner's share of the profits off the meter.

gestapo Another name for the 19 detectives hired by the fleet owners to patrol for taxi bandits performing flag ups.

graveyard shift The evening work shift. It is considered to be the most dangerous work period in the industry since most taxi robberies and murders occur on this shift. Consequently, it is labeled the graveyard shift.

gyps An expression used during the twenties and thirties to describe high priced taxicabs. "It was a gyp."

gypsy This generally refers to anyone who is not a medallioned taxi driver; however, in its broad interpretation, it covers all drivers (taxi drivers as well) operating illegally. Although the Taxi and Limousine Commission has tried to distinguish between gypsy cabs and public liveries, taxi drivers refuse to believe there is a distinction. They claim that the supposedly legal status of the public livery is really a sham since these operators are continually procuring business of the street.

hack beats A phrase used to describe a passenger who refused to pay the taxi driver his money. In other words, they beat the hack out of his money. It was commonly used at the turn of the century.

hack stand Curbside locations throughout the city where a hack can park and wait for a fare. Normally stands are found at hotels, terminals, and busy activity centers. In the early years of the industry there were private hack stands operated as concessions by the owner of the abutting property.

hot seat A pressure sensitive device under the passenger's seat which automatically triggers the meter within 20 seconds after the passenger has sat down.

icebergers Hacks who come to the airport in the early morning to make the first fare of the day a big one. Often this implies a big extortion on the part of the driver. Sometimes the method of procuring a big fare involves off seat solicitation or coercion within the airport terminals.

icebreakers See the definition of breaking the ice.

initial drop The first charge on the meter for hiring a taxi. The higher the initial drop, the more likely the driver will be to serve people on long trips.

inside men Fleet dispatchers. These men determine who will receive a taxi and which taxi he will drive. These men expect a kickback from all drivers for their favors.

jockeys The men who rode the running boards of the old New York taxis soliciting business for the driver and intimidating those who refused to submit to their extortionist manipulations. Jockeys were illegal after 1913; however, they continued as long as the automobile manufacturers produced taxis with running boards.

limousine bandits Those limousine services which gouge into the taxi business at airports and hotels within the city.

Motor Corporation A group of 19 detectives known as the Motor Corp. gestapo or rat squad hired by the owners to apprehend all fleet drivers riding the arm.

Mr. Big Another name for the inside men.

night hawks An old term describing drivers who worked the night shift. The connotation was that all night drivers were hawks preying on the defenseless citizens of New York.

omnipresence This is the key word used by the hack police in explaining the random and far from thorough inspection patterns throughout the city. The hack police want the drivers to feel that they might get caught performing a violation in any part of the city; however, drivers are not sold on the concept of omnipresence since they are aware of the very small number of locations in which the hack police omnipresently hang out.

production quota See booking quota.

rat squad See gestapo and Motor Corporation.

relief hack stand Curbside parking spots specifically designed for hacks taking lunch breaks or doing minor repairs on their taxis.

riding the arm When the driver rides with the arm or flag of the meter up. This is equivalent to a flag up violation.

riding the ghost See riding the arm.

rig Another name for a taxi. This word is an outgrowth of the original vehicle pulled by horses.

steerer The practice of soliciting customers for other businesses often of a disreputable nature.

stiff Any person who refuses to tip the cab driver.

taxicab jockeys See the definition of jockeys.

threw the flag The act of turning on the meter.

water rats See the definition of dock rats.

Bibliography

Adams, Alton D., "Cost and Limitations of Electric Vehicle Traction," *Scientific American*, July 28, 1900.

American Stock Exchange, *Yonkers Raceway, Inc.*, Listing Application No. 3790, March 20, 1961.

Board of Aldermen, City of New York, *Code of Ordinances*, May 27, 1913.

———, Report of Standing Committee Rec. No. 9, *Code of Ordinances*, March 24, 1925.

———, *Ordinance No. 99, The Haas Act*, March 9, 1937.

———, *Minutes of Public Hearings before the Committee on Taxicab Survey on Proposed Ordinance to Regulate the Taxicab Industry in the City of New York*, March 15–26 of 1934. Aldermanic stenographic minutes.

Board of Taxicab Control, *The Taxicab Code*, May 31, 1932, unpublished document.

Coleman, John A. *Committee Report on Taxi Tax*, October 20, 1959, New York unpublished document.

Coser, Lewis, *The Functions of Social Conflict*, New York: The Free Press, 1956.

Court of General Sessions, New York County, *People v. Cuneen*, March 1916.

City Magistrates Court of City of New York, *People v. Pfingst*, January 13, 1956.

Elliot, J. Richard, Jr., "All the Traffic Will Bear," *Barron's National Business and Financial Weekly*, September 10, 1962.

Greenleaf, William, *Monopoly on Wheels*, Detroit: Wayne State University Press, 1961.

Kennedy, Robert, *The Enemy Within*. New York, Harper and Row, Publishers, 1960.

Kitch, Edmund W. and others, "The Regulation of Taxicabs," *The Journal of Law and Economics*, Volume XIV, Chicago: The University of Chicago Law School, October, 1971.

184

Lazar, Michael, *The Non-Medallion Industry: A Transportation Phenomena,* City Record Supplement, November 19, 1971, New York City.

Ledesderff & Co., *Special Report with Respect to Fleet Owned Taxicabs,* December 1967, unpublished document.

Mayor's Committee on Taxicab Survey, *Report,* New York City, June 28, 1934, unpublished document.

Mayor's Taxi Study Panel, *Recommendations to John V. Lindsay,* December 1966, unpublished document.

Municipal Assembly, of the City of New York, *Business Requiring a License,* May 9, 1899.

——, *Local Law No. 31,* January 1931.

National Labor Relations Board, Region 29, *Carrick Service Co. and Taxi Drivers Organizing Committee,* November 16, 1965.

——, *Cab Operating Corp. and Taxi Drivers Organizing Committee and Local Union 826, International Brotherhood of Teamsters, Chauffeurs, Warehousemen and Helpers of America,* June 29, 1965.

New York Times, publications concerning the Taxicab Industry from 1896 to 1972.

Northrop, William, *The Insolence of Office: The Story of the Seabury Investigations.* New York: G. P. Putnam's Sons, 1932.

O'Connor, John E. *The Organization of Local 3036, New York City Taxi Union, AFL-CIO,* 1966 unpublished document.

Ornati, Oscar, *Transportation Needs of the Poor: A Case Study of New York City.* Praeger publishers, copyright 1969.

Perry, Harry W., "Taximeter Motor Cabs in America," *Scientific American,* November 9, 1907.

Price Waterhouse & Co., *New York City Fleet Taxicab Industry: Financial Survey,* September 1967, unpublished document.

——, *New York City Fleet Taxicab Industry: Financial Survey* June 30, 1970, unpublished document.

Report of Select Committee on Improper Activities in Labor or Management Field, *Senate Report No. 1417,* 85th Congress of the United States.

Rosenbloom, Sandra, "Taxis, Jitneys and Poverty," *Transaction,* February 1970.

Scientific American, *An Electric Hansom,* March 13, 1897.

——, *The Electric Cab Service of New York City,* March 25, 1899.

——, *Taximeter Frauds,* October 21, 1911.

Spiegelman, Jack, "Confessions of a New York Cabbie," *New York Magazine,* December 1970.

Spring 3100, The Magazine for Policemen, *Taxicab Truck Surveillance Unit,* March 1971.

Starr, Roger, "The Decline and Decline of New York," *New York Times Magazine,* November 21, 1971.

Supreme Court Special Term, New York County, *Yellow Taxicab v. Gaynor,* August 21, 1913.

Supreme Court Pre-Trial Term, New York County, *Teller v. Clear Service Co.,* March 6, 1958.

Taxi Committee, *Second Report on the Operation of the Health and Welfare Plan Created for the Eligible Employees in the New York City Taxicab Industry,* May 1967, unpublished document.

Taxicab Panel, *Report to Robert F. Wagner,* April 30, 1965, unpublished document.

Transportation Administration, *New York City Audit Report: Taxi Industry,* November 10, 1970.

Tri-State Transportation Commission, *Who Rides Taxis: A Regional Profile,* Volume 1, Number 11, February 1969.

United States District Court, Southern District, New York, *Mull v. Colt Co. Inc.,* 1962.

United States Senate Hearings, *Investigation of Improper Activities in the Labor or Management Field,* Volumes 10, 11, 12 and 13, 85th Congress, 1957.

Verkuil, Paul R., *The Economic Regulation of Taxicabs,* Rutgers Law Review, Volume 24, Summer 1970, Number 4, published by Rutgers University School of Law, Newark, New Jersey.

Vidich, Charles, *Off-the-Meter Negotiations: A Study of the New York Taxi Industry,* January 15, 1971, unpublished.

———, *Service Refusal in the Taxi Industry,* City Record Supplement, October 28, 1971, New York City.

Vidich, Paul, *The Economic Regulation of Taxicabs.* Thesis submitted to the faculty of Wesleyan University, May 1972, Middletown, Conn.

Walsh, Frank, *Report of the Mayor's Commission on Taxicabs,* New York City, September 23, 1930.

Whitman, Roger B., "Taximeter Frauds," *Scientific American,* January 30, 1909.

Figures